OVER THERE

War Scenes on the Western Front

By ARNOLD BENNETT

Originally published in 1915.

I The Zone Of Paris

From the balcony you look down upon massed and variegated tree- tops as though you were looking down upon a valley forest from a mountain height. Those trees, whose hidden trunks make alleys and squares, are rooted in the history of France. On the dusty gravel of the promenade which runs between the garden and the street a very young man and a girl, tiny figures, are playing with rackets at one of those second-rate ball games beloved by the French petite bourgeoisie. Their jackets and hats are hung on the corner of the fancy wooden case in which an orange-tree is planted. They are certainly perspiring in the heavy heat of the early morning. They are also certainly in love. This lively dalliance is the preliminary to a day's desk-work. It seems ill-chosen, silly, futile. The couple have forgotten, if they ever knew, that they are playing at a terrific and long-drawn moment of crisis in a spot sacred to the finest civilisation.

From the balcony you can see, close by, the Louvre, with its sculptures extending from Jean Goujon to Carpeaux; the Church of St. Clotilde, where Cesar Franck for forty years hid his genius away from popularity; the railway station of the Quai d'Orsay, which first proved that a terminus may excite sensations as fine as those excited by a palace or a temple; the dome of the Invalides; the unique facades, equal to any architecture of modern times, to the north of the Place de la Concorde, where the Ministry of Marine has its home. Nobody who knows Paris, and understands what Paris has meant and still means to humanity, can regard the scene without the most exquisite sentiments of humility, affection, and gratitude. It is impossible to look at the plinths, the mouldings, the carving of the Ministry of

Marine and not be thrilled by that supreme expression of national art.

And all this escaped! That is the feeling which one has. All this beauty was menaced with disaster at the hands of beings who comprehended it even less than the simple couple playing ball, beings who have scarcely reached the beginnings of comprehension, and who joined a barbaric ingenuousness to a savage cruelty. It was menaced, but it escaped. Perhaps no city was ever in acuter peril; it escaped by a miracle, but it did escape. It escaped because tens of thousands of soldiers in thousands of taxi- cabs advanced more rapidly than any soldiers could be expected to advance. "The population of Paris has revolted and is hurrying to ask mercy from us!" thought the reconnoitring simpletons in Taubes, when they noted beneath them the incredible processions of taxi- cabs going north. But what they saw was the Sixth Army, whose movement changed the campaign, and perhaps the whole course of history.

"A great misfortune has overtaken us," said a German officer the next day. It was true. Greater than he suspected.

The horror of what might have happened, the splendour of what did happen, mingle in the awed mind as you look over the city from the balcony. The city escaped. And the event seems vaster and more sublime than the mind can bear.

The streets of Paris have now a perpetual aspect of Sunday morning; only the sound of church-bells is lacking. A few of the taxi- cabs have come back; but all the auto-buses without exception are away behind the front. So that the traffic is forced underground, where the railways are manned by women. A horse-bus, dug up out of the past, jogs along the most famous boulevard in the world like a country diligence, with a fat, laughing peasant-woman clinging to its back-step and collecting fare-moneys into the immense pocket of her black apron. Many of the most expensive and unnecessary shops are shut; the others wait with strange meekness for custom. But the provision shops and all the sturdy cheap shops of the poor go on naturally, without any self-consciousness, just as usual. The pavements show chiefly soldiers in a wild, new variety of uniforms, from pale blue to black, imitated and adapted from all sources, and especially from England—and widows and orphans. The number of young girls and women in mourning, in the heavy mourning affected by the Latin race, is enormous. This crape is the sole casualty list permitted by the French War Office. It suffices. Supreme grief is omnipresent; but it is calm, cheerful, smiling. Widows glance at each other with understanding, like initiates of a secret and powerful society.

Never was Paris so disconcertingly odd. And yet never was it more profoundly itself. Between the slow realisation of a monstrous peril escaped and the equally slow realisation of its power to punish, the French spirit, angered and cold, knows at last what the French spirit is. And to watch and share its mood is positively ennobling to the stranger. Paris is revealed under an enchantment, On the surface of the enchantment the pettinesses of daily existence persist queerly.

Two small rooms and a kitchen on a sixth floor. You could put the kitchen, of which the cooking apparatus consists of two gas-rings, in the roots of the orange-tree in the Tuileries gardens. Everything is plain, and stringently tidy; everything is a special item, separately acquired, treasured. I see again a water-colour that I did years ago and had forgotten; it lives, protected by a glazed frame and by the pride of possession. The solitary mistress of this immaculate home is a spinster sempstress in the thirties. She earns three francs a day, and is rich because she does not spend it all, and has never spent it all. Inexpressibly neat, smiling, philosophic, helpful, she has within her a contentious and formidable tiger which two contingencies, and two only, will arouse. The first contingency springs from any threat of marriage. You must not seek a husband for her; she is alone in the world, and she wants to be. The second springs from any attempt to alter her habits, which in her sight are as sacredly immutable as the ritual of an Asiatic pagoda.

Last summer she went to a small town, to which is attached a very large military camp, to help her sister-in-law in the running of a cafe. The excursion was to be partly in the nature of a holiday; but, indefatigable on a chair with a needle, she could not stand for hours on her feet, ministering to a sex of which she knew almost nothing. She had the nostalgia of the Parisian garret. She must go home to her neglected habits. The war was waging. She delayed, from a sense of duty. But at last her habits were irresistible. Officers had said lightly that there was no danger, that the Germans could not possibly reach that small town. Nevertheless, the train that the spinster-sempstress took was the last train to leave. And as the spinster-sempstress departed by the train, so the sister-in-law departed in a pony-cart, with a son and a grandmother in the pony- cart, together with such goods as the cart would hold; and, through staggering adventures, reached safety at Troyes.

"And how did you yourself get on?" I asked the spinster-sempstress.

She answered:

"It was terrible. Ordinarily it is a journey of three or four hours. But that time it lasted three days and two nights. The train was crammed with refugees and with wounded. One was obliged to stand up. One could not move."

"But where did you sleep?"

"I did not sleep. Do I not tell you one was obliged to stand up? I stood up all the first night. The floor was thirty centimetres deep in filth. The second night one had settled down somewhat. I could sit."

"But about eating?"

"I had a little food that I brought with me."

"And drinking?"

"Nothing, till the second day. One could not move. But in the end we arrived. I was broken with fatigue. I was very ill. But I was home. The Boches drank everything in the cafe, everything; but the building was spared—it stood away from the firing. How long do you think the war will last?"

"I'm beginning to think it will last a long time."

"So they say," she murmured, glancing through the window at the prospect of roofs and chimney-cowls. "Provided that it finishes well…"

Except by the look in her eyes, and by the destruction of her once good complexion, it was impossible to divine that this woman's habits had ever been disturbed in the slightest detail. But the gaze and the complexion told the tale.

Next: the Boulevard St. Germain. A majestic flat, heavily and sombrely furnished. The great drawing-room is shut and sheeted with holland. It has been shut for twenty years. The mistress of this home is an aged widow of inflexible will and astounding activity. She gets up at five a.m., and no cook has ever yet satisfied her. The master is her son, a bachelor of fifty. He is paralysed, and always perfectly dressed in the English taste, he passes his life in a wheeled chair. The home is centred in his study, full of books, engravings, a large safe, telephone, theatrophone, newspapers, cigarettes, easy-chairs. When I go in, an old friend, a stockbroker, is there, and "thees" and "thous" abound in the conversation, which runs on investments, the new English loan, banking accounts in London, the rent moratorium in Paris, and the war. It is said that every German is a critic of war. But so is every Frenchman a critic of war. The criticism I now hear is the best spoken criticism, utterly impartial, that I have heard.

"In sum," says the grey-headed stockbroker, "there disengages itself from the totality of the facts an impression, tolerably clear, that all goes very well on the West front."

Which is reassuring. But the old lady, invincible after seven-and-a-half decades spent in the hard acquirement of wisdom, will not be reassured. She is not alarmed, but she will not be reassured. She treats the two men with affectionate malice as children. She knows that "those birds"—that is to say, the Germans—will never be beaten, because they are for ever capable of inventing some new trick.

She will not sit still. A bit of talk, and she runs off with the agility of a girl to survey her household; then returns and cuts into the discussion.

"If you are coming to lunch, Bennett," she says, "come before Monday, because on Monday my cook takes herself away, and as for the new one, I should dare to say nothing. . . . You don't know, Bennett, you don't know, that at a given moment it was impossible to buy salt. I mean, they sold it to you unwillingly, in little screws of paper. It was impossible to get enough. Figure that to yourself, you from London! As for chicory for the morning cafe-au-lait, it existed not. Gold could not buy it."

And again she said, speaking of the fearful days in September 1914:

"What would you? We waited. My little coco is nailed there. He cannot move without a furniture-van filled with things essential to his existence. I did not wish to move. We waited, quite simply. We waited for them to come. They did not come. So much the better That is all."

I have never encountered anything more radically French than the temperament of this aged woman.

Next: the luxury quarter—the establishment of one of those fashionable dressmakers whom you patronise, and whose bills startle all save the most hardened. She is a very handsome woman. She has a husband and two little boys. They are all there. The husband is a retired professional soldier. He has a small and easy post in a civil administration, but his real work is to keep his wife's books. In August he was re-engaged, and ready to lead soldiers under fire in the fortified camp which Gallieni has evolved out of the environs of Paris; but the need passed, and the uniform was laid aside. The two little boys are combed and dressed as only French and American children are combed and dressed, and with a more economical ingenuity than American children. Each has a beautiful purple silk necktie and a beautiful silk handkerchief to match. You may notice that the purple silk is exactly the same purple silk as the lining of their mother's rich mantle hanging over a chair back.

"I had to dismiss my last few work-girls on Saturday," said the dressmaker. It was no longer possible to keep them. "I had seventy, you know. Now—not one. For a time we made considerably less than the rent. Now we make nothing. Nevertheless, some American clients have been very kind."

Her glance went round the empty white salons with their mirrors in sculptured frames. Naught of her stock was left except one or two fragile blouses and a few original drawings.

Said the husband:

"We are eating our resources. I will tell you what this war means to us. It means that we shall have to work seven or eight years longer than we had the intention to work. What would you?"

He lifted his arms and lowered the corners of his mouth. Then he turned again to the military aspect of things, elaborating it.

The soldier in him finished:

"It is necessary, all the same, to admire these cursed Germans."

"Admire them!" said his wife sharply. "I do not appreciate the necessity. When I think of that day and that night we spent at home!" They live in the eastern suburbs of the city. "When I think of that day and that night! The cannon thundering at a distance of ten kilometres!"

"Thirty kilometres, almost thirty, my friend," the husband corrected.

"Ten kilometres. I am sure it was not more than ten kilometres, my friend."

"But see, my little one. It was at Meaux. Forty kilometres to Meaux.

We are at thirteen. That makes twenty-seven, at least."

"It sounded like ten."

"That is true."

"It sounded like ten, my dear Arnold. All day, and all night. We could not go to bed. Had one any desire to go to bed? It was anguish. The mere souvenir is anguish."

She kissed her youngest boy, who had long hair.

"Come, come!" the soldier calmed her.

Lastly: an interior dans le monde; a home illustrious in Paris for the richness of its collections—bric-a-brac, fans, porcelain, furniture, modern pictures; the walls frescoed by

Pierre Bonnard and his compeers; a black marble balcony with an incomparable view in the very middle of the city. Here several worlds encountered each other: authors, painters, musicians, dilettanti, administrators. The hostess had good-naturedly invited a high official of the Foreign Office, whom I had not seen for many years; she did not say so, but her aim therein was to expedite the arrangements for my pilgrimages in the war-zone. Sundry of my old friends were present. It was wonderful how many had escaped active service, either because they were necessary to central administration, or because they were neutrals, or because they were too old, or because they had been declined on account of physical unfitness, reformes. One or two who might have come failed to do so because they had perished.

Amid the abounding, dazzling confusion of objects which it was a duty to admire, people talked cautiously of the war. With tranquillity and exactness and finality the high official, clad in pale alpaca and yellow boots, explained the secret significance of Yellow Books, White Books, Orange Books, Blue Books. The ultimate issues were never touched. New, yet unprinted, music was played; Schumann, though German enough, was played. Then literature came to the top. A novelist wanted to know what I thought of a book called "The Way of All Flesh," which he had just read. It is singular how that ruthless book makes its way across all frontiers. He also wanted to know about Gissing, a name new to him. And then a voice from the obscurity of the balcony came startlingly to me in the music-room:

"Tell me! Sincerely—do they hate the Germans in England? Do they hate them, veritably? Tell me. I doubt it. I doubt strongly."

I laughed, rather awkwardly, as any Englishman would.

The transient episode was very detrimental to literary talk.

Negotiations for a private visit to the front languished. The thing was arranged right enough, but it seemed impossible to fix a day actually starting. So I went to Meaux. Meaux had stuck in my ears. Meaux was in history and in romances; it is in Dumas. It was burnt by the Normans in the tenth century, and terrific massacres occurred outside its walls in the fourteenth century, massacres in which the English aristocracy took their full share of the killing. Also, in the seventeenth century, Bossuet was Bishop of Meaux. Finally, in the twentieth century, the Germans just got to Meaux, and they got no further. It was, so far as I can make out, the nearest point to Paris which they soiled.

I could not go even to Meaux without formalities, but the formalities were simple. The dilatory train took seventy minutes, dawdling along the banks of the notorious Marne. In an automobile one could have done the journey in half the time. An automobile, however, would have seriously complicated the formalities. Meaux contains about fourteen thousand inhabitants. Yet it seems, when you are in it, to' consist chiefly of cathedral. When you are at a little distance away from it, it seems to consist of nothing but cathedral. In this it resembles Chartres, and many another city in France.

We obtained a respectable carriage, with a melancholy, resigned old driver, who said:

"For fifteen francs, plus always the pourboire, I will take you to Barcy, which was bombarded and burnt. I will show you all the battlefield."

With those few words he thrilled me.

The road rose slowly from the canal of the Ourcq; it was lined with the most beautiful acacia trees, and through the screen of the acacias one had glimpses of the town, diminishing, and of the cathedral, growing larger and larger. The driver talked to us in faint murmurs over his shoulder, indicating the positions of various villages such as Penchard, Poincy, Crecy, Monthyon, Chambry, Varreddes, all of which will be found, in the future detailed histories of the great locust-advance.

"Did you yourself see any Germans?"

"Yes."

"Where?"

"At Meaux."

"How many?"

He smiled. "About a dozen." He underestimated the number, and the length of the stay, but no matter. "They were scouts. They came into the town for a few hours—and left it. The Germans were deceived. They might have got to Paris if they had liked. But they were deceived."

"How were they deceived?"

"They thought there were more English in front of them than actually there were. The head-quarters of the English were over there, at La Ferte-sous-Jouarre. The English blew up our bridge, as a measure of precaution."

We drove on.

"The first tomb," said the driver, nonchalantly, in his weak voice, lifting an elbow.

There it was, close by the roadside, and a little higher than ourselves. The grave was marked by four short, rough posts on which was strung barbed wire; a white flag; a white cross of painted wood, very simply but neatly made; a faded wreath. We could distinguish a few words of an inscription. "Comrades, 66th Territorials…" Soldiers were buried where they fell, and this was the tomb of him who fell nearest to Paris. It marked the last homicidal effort of the Germans before their advance in this region curved eastwards into a retreat. This tomb was a very impressive thing. The driver had thrilled me again.

We drove on. We were now in a large rolling plain that sloped gradually behind us southwards towards the Marne. It had many little woods and spinneys, and no watercourses. To the civilian it ap- peared an ideal theatre for a glorious sanguinary battle in which thousands of fathers, sons, and brothers should die violently because some hierarchy in a distant capital was suffering from an acute attack of swelled head. A few trenches here and there could still be descried, but the whole land was in an advanced state of cultivation. Wheat and oats and flaming poppies had now conquered the land, had overrun and possessed it as no Germans could ever do. The raw earth of the trenches struggled vainly against the tide of germination. The harvest was going to be good. This plain, with its little woods and little villages, glittered with a careless and vast satisfaction in the sheets of sunshine that fell out of a blue too intense for the gaze.

We saw a few more tombs, and a great general monument or cenotaph to the dead, constructed at cross-roads by military engineers. The driver pointed to the village of Penchard, which had been pillaged and burnt by the enemy. It was only about a mile off, but in the strong, dazzling light we could distinguish not the least sign of damage. Then we came to a farm-house by the roadside. It was empty; it was a shell, and its roof was damaged. The Germans had gutted it. They had taken away its furniture as booty. (What they intended to do with furniture out of a perfectly mediocre farm-house, hundreds of miles from home, it is difficult to imagine.) Articles which it did not suit them to carry off they destroyed. Wine-casks of which they could not drink the wine, they stove in. ... And then they retreated.

This farm-house was somebody's house, just as your home is yours, and mine mine. To some woman or other every object in it was familiar. She glanced at the canister on the mantelpiece and said to herself: "I really must clean that canister to-morrow." There the house stood, with holes in its roof, empty. And if there are half a million similarly tragic houses in Europe to-day, as probably there are, such frequency does not in the slightest degree diminish the forlorn tragedy of that particular house which I have beheld.

At last Barcy came into view—the pierced remains of its church tower over the brow of a rise in the plain. Barcy is our driver's show- place. Barcy was in the middle of things. The fighting round Barcy lasted a night and a day, and Barcy was taken and retaken twice.

"You see the new red roofs," said the driver as we approached. "By those new red roofs you are in a state to judge a little what the damage was."

Some of the newly made roofs, however, were of tarred paper.

The street by which we entered had a small-pox of shrapnel and bullet-marks. The post office had particularly suffered: its bones were laid bare. It had not been restored, but it was ready to do any business that fell to be done, though closed on that afternoon. We turned a corner, and came upon the church. The work on the church was well up to the reported Teutonic average. Of its roof only the rafters were left. The windows were all smashed, and their lead fantastically twisted. The west door was entirely gone; a rough grille of strips of wood served in its stead. Through this grille one could see the nave and altar, in a miraculous and horrible confusion. It was as if house-breakers had spent days in doing their best to produce a professional effect. The oak pews were almost unharmed. Immediately behind the grille lay a great bronze bell, about three feet high, covered with beautifully incised inscriptions; it was unhurt.

Apparently nothing had been accomplished, in ten months, towards the restoration of the church. But something was contemplated, perhaps already started. A polished steel saw lay on one of the pews, but there was no workman attached to it.

While I was writing some notes in the porch three little boys came up and diligently stared at me.

"What dost thou want?" I said sharply to the tallest.

"Nothing," he replied.

Then three widows came up, one young, one young and beautiful, one middle-aged.

We got back into the carriage.

"The village seems very deserted," I said to the driver.

"What would you?" he answered. "Many went. They had no home. Few have returned."

All around were houses of which nothing remained but the stone walls.

The Germans had shown great prowess here, and the French still greater. It was a village upon which rival commanders could gaze with pride. It will remember the fourth and the fifth of September 1914.

We made towards Chambry. Chambry is a village which, like Meaux, lies below the plain. Chambry escaped glory; but between it and Barcy, on the intervening slope through which a good road runs, a battle was fought. You know what kind of a battle it was by the tombs. These tombs were very like the others—an oblong of barbed wire, a white flag, a white cross, sometimes a name, more often only a number, rarely a wreath. You see first one, then another, then two, then a sprinkling; and gradually you perceive that the whole plain is dotted with gleams of white flags and white crosses, so that graves seem to extend right away to the horizon marked by lines of trees. Then you see a huge general grave. Much glory about that spot!

And then a tomb with a black cross. Very disconcerting, that black cross! It is different not only in colour, but in shape, from the other crosses. Sinister! You need not to be told that the body of a German lies beneath it. The whole devilishness of the Prussian ideal is expressed in that black cross. Then, as the road curves, you see more black crosses, many black crosses, very many. No flags, no names, no wreaths on these tombs. Just a white stencilled number in the centre of each cross. Women in Germany are still lying awake at nights and wondering what those tombs look like.

Watching over all the tombs, white and black without distinction, are notices: "Respect the Tombs." But the wheat and the oats are not respecting the tombs. Everywhere the crops have encroached on them, half-hiding them, smothering them, climbing right over them. In one place wheat is ripening out of the very body of a German soldier.

Such is the nearest battlefield to Paris. Corporate excursions to it are forbidden, and wisely. For the attraction of the place, were it given play, would completely demoralise Meaux and the entire district.

In half an hour we were back at an utterly matter-of-fact railway station, in whose cafe an utterly matter-of-fact and capable Frenchwoman gave us tea. And when we reached Paris we had the news that a Staff Captain of the French Army had been detailed to escort us to the front and to show us all that could safely be seen. Nevertheless, whatever I may experience, I shall not experience again the thrill which I had when the weak and melancholy old driver pointed out the first tomb. That which we had just seen was the front once.

## II On The French Front

We were met at a poste de commandement by the officers in charge, who were waiting for us. And later we found that we were always thus met. The highest officer present—General, Colonel, or Commandant—was at every place at our disposition to explain things—and to explain them with that clarity of which the French alone have the secret and of which a superlative example exists in the official report of the earlier phases of the war, offered to the Anglo-Saxon public through Reuter. Automobiles and chauffeurs abounded for our small party of four. Never once at any moment of the day, whether driving furiously along somewhat deteriorated roads in the car, or walking about the land, did I lack a Staff officer who produced in me the illusion that he was living solely in order to be of use to me. All details of the excursions were elaborately organised; never once did the organisation break down. No pre- Lusitania American correspondent could have been more spoiled by Germans desperately anxious for his goodwill than I was spoiled by these French who could not gain my goodwill because they had the whole of it already. After the rites of greeting, we walked up to the high terrace of a considerable chateau close by, and France lay before us in a shimmering vast semicircle. In the distance, a low range of hills, irregularly wooded; then a river; then woods and spinneys; then vineyards—boundless vineyards which climbed in varying slopes out of the valley almost to our feet. Far to the left was a town with lofty factory chimneys, smokeless.

Peasant women were stooping in the vineyards; the whole of the earth seemed to be cultivated and to be yielding bounteously. It was a magnificent summer afternoon. The sun was high and a few huge purple shadows moved with august deliberation across the brilliant greens. An impression of peace, majesty, grandeur; and of the mild, splendid richness of the soil of France.

"You see that white line on the hills opposite," said an officer, opening a large-scale map.

I guessed it was a level road.

"That is the German trenches," said he. "They are five miles away. Their gun-positions are in the woods. Our own trenches are invisible from here."

It constituted a great moment, this first vision of the German trenches. With the thrill came the lancinating thought: "All of France that lies beyond that line, land just like the land on which I am standing, inhabited by people just like the people who are talking to me, is under the insulting tyranny of the invader." And I also thought, as the sense of distance quickened my imagination to realise that these trenches stretched from Ostend to Switzerland, and that the creators of them were prosecuting similar enterprises as far north-east as Riga, and as far southeast as the confines of Roumania: "The brigands are mad, but they are mad in the grand manner."

We were at the front.

We had driven for twenty miles along a very busy road which was closed to civilians, and along which even Staff officers could not travel without murmuring the password to placate the hostile vigilance of sentries. The civil life of the district was in abeyance, proceeding precariously from meal to meal. Aeroplanes woke the sleep. No letter could leave a post office without a precautionary delay of three days.

Telegrams were suspect. To get into a railway station was almost as difficult as to get into paradise. A passport or a safe-conduct was the sine qua non of even the restricted liberty which had survived. And yet nowhere did I see a frown nor hear a complaint. Everybody comprehended that the exigencies of the terrific military machine were necessary exigencies. Everybody waited, waited, in confidence and with tranquil smiles. Also it is misleading to say that civil life was in abeyance. For the elemental basis of its prosperity and its amenities continued just as though the lunatic bullies of Potsdam had never dictated to Vienna the ultimatum for Serbia. The earth was yielding, fabulously. It was yielding up to within a mile and a half of the German wire entanglements. The peasants would not neglect the earth. Officers remonstrated with them upon their perilous rashness. They replied: "The land must be tilled."

When the German artillery begins to fire, the blue-clad women sink out of sight amid the foliage. Half an hour after it has ceased they cautiously emerge, and resume. One peasant put up an umbrella, but he was a man.

We were veritably at the front. There was, however, not a whisper of war, nor anything visible except the thin, pale line like a striation on the distant hills. Then a far-off sound of thunder is heard. It is a gun. A faint puff of smoke is pointed out to us. Neither the rumble nor the transient cloudlet makes any apparent impression on the placid and wide dignity of the scene. Nevertheless, this is war. And war seems a very vague, casual, and negligible thing. We are led about fifty feet to the left, where in a previous phase a shell has indented a huge hole in the earth. The sight of this hole renders war rather less vague and rather less negligible.

"There are eighty thousand men in front of us," says an officer, indicating the benign shimmering, empty landscape.

"But where?"

"Interred—in the trenches."

It is incredible.

"And the other interred—the dead?"

I ask.

"We never speak of them. But we think of them a good deal."

Still a little closer to war. The parc du genie—engineers park. BEHIND We inspected hills of coils, formidable barbed wire, far surpassing that of farmers, well contrived to tear to pieces any human being who, having got into its entanglement, should try to get out again. One thought that nothing but steam-chisels would be capable of cutting it. Also stacks of timber for shoring up mines which sappers would dig beneath the enemy trenches. Also sacks to be filled with earth for improvised entrenching. Also the four-pointed contraptions called chevaux de frise, which—however you throw them—will always stick a fatal point upwards, to impale the horse or man who cannot or will not look where he is going. Even tarred paper, for keeping the weather out of trenches or anything else. And all these things in unimagined quantities.

Close by, a few German prisoners performing sanitary duties under a guard. They were men in God's image, and they went about on the assumption that all the rest of the war lay before them and that there was a lot of it. A General told us that he had mentioned to them the possibility of an exchange of prisoners, whereupon they had gloomily and pathetically protested. They very sincerely did not want to go back whence they had come, preferring captivity, humiliation, and the basest tasks to a share in the great glory of German arms. To me they had a brutalised air, no doubt one minor consequence of military ambition in high places.

Not many minutes away was a hospital—what the French call an ambulance de premiere ligne, contrived out of a factory. This was the hospital nearest to the trenches in that region, and the wounded come to it direct from the dressing-stations which lie immediately behind the trenches. When a man falls, or men fall, the automobile is telephoned for, and it arrives at the appointed rendezvous generally before the stretcher-bearers, who may have to walk for twenty or thirty minutes over rough ground. A wounded man may be, and has been, operated upon in this hospital within an hour of his wounding. It is organised on a permanent basis, for cases too serious for removal have, of course, to remain there. Nevertheless, these establishments are, as regards their staff, patients, and material, highly mobile.

One hospital of two hundred beds was once entirely evacuated within sixty minutes upon a sudden order. We walked through small ward after small ward, store-room after store-room, aseptic operating-room and septic operating-room, all odorous with ether, and saw little but resignation, and not much of that, for patients happened to be few. Yet the worn face of the doctor in charge showed that vast labours must have been accomplished in those sombre chambers.

In the very large courtyard a tent operating-hospital was established. The white attendants were waiting within in the pallid obscurity, among tables, glass jars, and instruments. The surgeon's wagon, with hot-water and sterilising apparatus, was waiting without. The canvas organism was a real hospital, and the point about it was that it could move off complete at twenty-five minutes' notice and set itself up again in any other ordained location in another twenty-five minutes.

Another short ride, and we were in an aviation park, likewise tented, in the midst of an immense wheatfield on the lofty side of a hill. There were six hangars of canvas, each containing an aeroplane and serving as a dormitory; and for each aeroplane a carriage and a motor—for sometimes aeroplanes are wounded and have to travel by road; it takes ninety minutes to dismount an aeroplane. Each corps of an army has one of these escadrilles or teams of aeroplanes, and the army as a whole has an extra one, so that, if an army consists of eight corps, it possesses fifty-four aeroplanes. I am speaking now of the particular type of aeroplane employed for regulating artillery fire. It was a young non-commissioned officer with a marked Southern accent who explained to us the secret nature of things. He was wearing both the Military Medal and the Legion of Honour, for he had done wondrous feats in the way of shooting the occupants of Taubes in mid-air. He got out one of the machines, and exhibited its tricks and its wireless apparatus, and invited us to sit in the seat of the flier. The weather was quite unsuitable for flying, but, setting four men to hold the machine in place, he started the Gnome motor and ran it up to two thousand revolutions a minute, creating a draught which bowed the fluttered wheat for many yards behind and blew hats off. And in the middle of this pother he continued to offer lucid and surprising explanations to deafened ears until his superior officer, excessively smart and looking like a cross between a cavalryman and a yachtsman, arrived on the scene swinging a cane.

It was natural that after this we should visit some autocannons expressly constructed for bringing down aeroplanes. In front of these marvels it was suggested to us that we should neither take photographs nor write down exact descriptions. As regards the latter, the Staff officers had reason to be reassured. No living journalist could have reproduced the scientific account of the sighting arrangements given to us in an esoteric yet quite comprehensible language by the high priest of these guns, who was a middle-aged artillery Captain. It lasted about twenty minutes. It was complete, final, unchallengeable. At intervals the artillery Captain himself admitted that such-and-such a part of the device was tres beau. It was. There was only one word of which I could not grasp the significance in that connection. It recurred. Several times I determined to ask the Captain what he meant us to understand by that word; but I lacked moral courage. I doubt whether in all the lethal apparatus that I saw in France I saw anything quite equal to the demoniac ingenuity of these massive guns. The proof of guns is in the shooting. These guns do not merely aim at Taubes: they hit them.

I will not, however, derogate from the importance of the illustrious "seventy-five." We saw one of these on an afternoon of much marching up and down hills and among woods, gazing at horses and hot-water douches, baths, and barbers' shops, and deep dug-outs called "Tipperary," and guns of various calibre, including the "seventy-five." The "seventy-five" is a very sympathetic creature, in blue-grey with metallic glints. He is perfectly easy to see when you approach him from behind, but get twenty yards in front of him and he is absolutely undiscoverable. Viewed from the sky, he is part of the forest. Viewed from behind, he is perceived to be in a wooden hut with rafters, in which you can just stand upright. We beheld the working of the gun, by two men, and we beheld the different sorts of shell in their delved compartments. But this was not enough for us. We ventured to suggest that it would be proper to try to kill a few Germans for our amusement. The request was instantly granted.

"Time for 4,300 metres," said the Lieutenant quickly and sternly, and a soldier manipulated the obus.

It was done. It was done with disconcerting rapidity. The shell was put into its place. A soldier pulled a string. Bang! A neat, clean, not too loud bang! The messenger had gone invisibly forth. The prettiest part of the affair was the recoil and automatic swinging back of the gun. Lest the first shell should have failed in its mission, the Commandant ordered a second one to be sent, and this time the two artillerymen sat in seats attached on either side to the gun itself. The "seventy-five" was enthusiastically praised by every officer present. He is beloved like a favourite sporting dog, and with cause.

At the side of the village street there was a bit of sharply sloping ground, with a ladder thrown on it to make descent easier. "This way," said one of the officers.

We followed him, and in an instant were in the communication trench. The change was magical in its quickness. At one moment we were on the earth; at the next we were in it. The trench was so narrow that I had to hold my stick in front of me, as there was no room to swing the arms; the chalky sides left traces on the elbows. The floor was for the most part quite dry, but at intervals there were muddy pools nearly ankle-deep. The top of the trench was about level with the top of my head, and long grasses or chance cereals, bending down, continually brushed the face. An officer was uplifted for the rest of the day by finding a four-leaved clover at the edge of the trench. The day was warm, and the trench was still warmer. Its direction never ceased to change, generally in curves, but now and then by a sharp corner. We walked what seemed to be an immense distance, and then came out on to a road, which we were instructed to cross two by two, as, like the whole of the region, it was subject to German artillery. Far down this road we could see the outlying village for which we were bound. . . .

A new descent into the earth. We proceed a few yards, and the trench suddenly divides into three. We do not know which to take. An officer following us does not know which to take. The guiding officer is perhaps thirty yards in front! We call. No answer. We climb out of the trench on to the surface desolation; we can see nothing, nothing whatever, but land that is running horribly to waste. Our friends are as invisible as moles. There is not a trace even of their track. This is a fine object-lesson in the efficacy of trenches. At length an officer returns and saves us. We have to take the trench on the extreme right. Much more hot walking, and a complete loss of the notion of direction.

Then we come out on to another portion of the same road at the point where a main line of railway crosses it. We are told to run to shelter. In the near distance a German captive balloon sticks up moveless against the sky. The main line of railway is a sorrowful sight. Its signal-wires hang in festoons. Its rails are rusting. The abandonment of a main line in a civilised country is a thing unknown, a thing contrary to sense, an impossible thing, so that one wonders whether one is not visiting the remains of a civilisation dead and definitely closed. Very strange thoughts pass through the mind. That portion of the main line cannot be used by the Germans because it is within the French positions, and it cannot be used by the French because it is utterly exposed to German artillery. Thus, perhaps ten kilometres of it are left forlorn to illustrate the imbecile brutality of an invasion. There is a good deal more trench before we reach the village which forms the head of a salient in the French line. This village is knocked all to pieces. It is a fearful spectacle. We see a Teddy-bear left on what remains of a flight of stairs, a bedstead buried to the knobs in debris, skeletons of birds in a cage hanging under an eave. The entire place is in the zone of fire, and it has been tremendously bombarded throughout the war. Nevertheless, some houses still stand, and seventeen civilians— seven men and ten women—insist on remaining there. I talked to one fat old woman, who contended that there was no danger. A few minutes later a shell fell within a hundred yards of her, and it might just as well have fallen on the top of her coiffe, to prove finally to her the noble reasonableness of war and the reality of the German necessity for expansion.

The village church was laid low. In the roof two thin arches of the groining remain, marvellously. One remembers this freak of balance—and a few poor flowers on the altar. Mass is celebrated in that church every Sunday morning. We spoke with the cure, an extremely emaciated priest of middle age; he wore the Legion of Honour. We took to the trenches again, having in the interval been protected by several acres of ruined masonry. About this point geography seemed to end for me. I was in a maze of burrowing, from which the hot sun could be felt but not seen. I saw stencilled signs, such as "Tranchee de repli," and signs containing numbers. I saw a sign over a door: "Guetteur de jour et de nuit"—watcher by day and by night.

"Anybody in there?"

"Certainly."

The door was opened. In the gloom a pale man stood rather like a ghost, almost as disconcerting as a ghost, watching. He ignored us, and kept on watching.

Then through a hole I had a glimpse of an abandoned road, where no man might live, and beyond it a vast wire entanglement. Then we curved, and I was in an open place, a sort of redoubt contrived out of little homes and cattle-stables. I heard irregular rifle-fire close by, but I could not see who was firing I was shown the machine-gun chamber, and the blind which hides the aperture for the muzzle was lifted, but only momentarily. I was shown, too, the deep underground refuges to which every body takes in case of a heavy bombardment. Then we were in the men's quarters, in houses very well protected by advance walls to the north, and at length we saw some groups of men.

"Bonjour, les poilus!"

This from the Commandant himself, with jollity. The Commandant had a wonderful smile, which showed bright teeth, and his gestures were almost as quick as those of his Lieutenant, whom the regiment had christened "The Electric Man."

The soldiers saluted. This salute was so proud, so eager, that it might have brought tears to the eyes. The soldiers stood up very straight, but not at all stiffly. I noticed one man, because I could not notice them all. He threw his head back, and slightly to one side, and his brown beard stuck out. His eyes sparkled. Every muscle was taut. He seemed to be saying, "My Commandant, I know my worth; I am utterly yours—you won't get anything better." A young officer said to me that these men had in them a wild beast and an angel. It was a good saying, and I wished I had thought of it myself. This regiment had been in this village since the autumn. It had declined to be relieved. It seemed absolutely fresh.

One hears that individual valour is about the same in all armies— everywhere very high. Events appear to have justified the assertion. German valour is astounding. I have not seen any German regiment, but I do not believe that there are in any German regiment any men equal to these men. After all, ideas must count, and these men know that they are defending an outraged country, while the finest German soldier knows that he is outraging it.

The regiment was relatively very comfortable. It had plenty of room. It had made a little garden, with little terra-cotta statues. It possessed also a gymnasium ground, where we witnessed some excellent high jumping; and—more surprising—a theatre, with stage, dressing-room, and women's costumes.

The summit of our excitement was attained when we were led into the first-line trench.

"Is this really the first-line trench?"

"It is."

Well, the first-line trench, very remarkably swept and dusted and spotless—as were all the trenches beyond the communication trench—was not much like a trench. It was like a long wooden gallery. Its sides were of wood, its ceiling was of wood, its floor was of wood. The carpentry, though not expert, was quite neat; and we were told that not a single engineer had ever been in the position, which, nevertheless, is reckoned to be one of the most ingenious on the whole front. The gallery is rather dark, because it is lighted only by the loop-holes. These loop-holes are about eight inches square, and more than eight inches deep, because they must, of course, penetrate the outer earthwork. A couple of inches from the bottom a strong wire is fixed across them. At night the soldier puts his gun under this wire, so that he may not fire too high.

The loop-holes are probably less than a yard apart, allowing enough space in front of each for a man to move comfortably. Beneath the loop-holes runs a wooden platform for the men to stand on. Behind the loop-holes, in the ceiling, are large hooks to hang guns on. Many of the loop-holes are labelled with men's names, written in a good engrossing hand; and between the loop-holes, and level with them, are pinned coloured postcards and photographs of women, girls, and children. Tucked conveniently away in zinc cases underground are found zinc receptacles for stores of cartridges, powders to be used against gas, grenades, and matches.

One gazes through a loop-hole. Occasional firing can be heard, but it is not in the immediate vicinity. Indeed, all the men we can see have stepped down from the platform in order to allow us to pass freely along it and inspect. Through the loop-hole can be distinguished a barbed-wire entanglement, then a little waste ground, then more barbed-wire entanglement (German), and then the German trenches, which are less than half a mile away, and which stretch round behind us in a semicircle.

"Do not look too long. They have very good glasses."

The hint is taken. It is singular to reflect that just as we are gazing privily at the Germans, so the Germans are gazing privily at us. A mere strip of level earth separates them from us, but that strip is impassable, save at night, when the Frenchmen often creep up to the German wire. There is a terrible air of permanency about the whole affair. Not only the passage of time produces this effect; the telephone-wire running along miles of communication-trench, the elaborateness of the fighting trenches, the established routine and regularity of existence—all these also contribute to it. But the air of permanency is fallacious. The Germans are in France.

Every day of slow preparation brings nearer the day when the Germans will not be in France. That is certain. An immense expectancy hangs over the land, enchanting it.

We leave the first-line trench, with regret. But we have been in it!

In the quarters of the Commandant, a farm-house at the back end of the village, champagne was served, admirable champagne. We stood round a long table, waiting till the dilatory should have arrived. The party had somehow grown. For example, the cure came, amid acclamations. He related how a Lieutenant had accosted him in front of some altar and asked whether he might be allowed to celebrate the Mass. "That depends," said the cure. "You cannot celebrate if you are not a priest. If you are, you can." "I am a priest," said the Lieutenant. And he celebrated the Mass. Also the Intendant came, a grey-haired, dour, kind-faced man. The Intendant has charge of supplies, and he is cherished accordingly. And in addition to the Commandant, and the Electric Man, and our Staff Captains, there were sundry non-commissioned officers, and even privates.

We were all equal. The French Army is by far the most democratic institution I have ever seen. On our journeys the Staff Captains and ourselves habitually ate with a sergeant and a corporal. The corporal was the son of a General. The sergeant was a man of business and a writer. His first words when he met me were in English: "Monsieur Bennett, I have read your books." One of our chauffeurs was a well-known printer who employs three hundred and fifty men—when there is peace. The relations between officers and men are simply unique. I never saw a greeting that was not exquisite. The officers w ere full of knowledge, decision, and appreciative kindliness. The men were bursting with eager devotion. This must count, perhaps even more than big guns.

The Commandant, of course, presided at the vin d'honneur. His glance and his smile, his latent energy, would have inspired devotion in a wooden block. Every glass touched every glass, an operation which entailed some threescore clinkings. And while we were drinking, one of the Staff Captains—the one whose English was the less perfect of the two—began to tell me of the career of the Commandant, in Algeria and elsewhere. Among other things, he had carried his wounded men on his own shoulders under fire from the field of battle to a place of safety. He was certainly under forty; he might have been under thirty-five.

Said the Staff Captain, ingenuously translating in his mind from French to English, and speaking with slow caution, as though picking his way among the chevaux de frise of the English language:

"There are—very beautiful pages—in his—military life."

He meant: "Il y a de tres belles pages dans sa carriere militaire."

Which is subtly not quite the same thing.

As we left the farm-house to regain the communication trench there was a fierce, loud noise like this: ZZZZZ ssss ZZZZ sss ZZZZ. And then an explosion. The observer in the captive balloon had noticed unaccustomed activity in our village, and the consequences were coming. We saw yellow smoke rising just beyond the wall of the farmyard, about two hundred yards away. We received instructions to hurry to the trench. We had not gone fifty yards in the trench when there was another celestial confusion of S's and Z's. Imitating the officers, we bent low in the trench. The explosion followed.

"One, two, three, four, five," said a Captain. "One should not rise till one has counted five, because all the bits have not fallen. If it is a big shell, count ten."

We tiptoed and glanced over the edge of the trench. Yellow smoke was rising at a distance of about three lawn-tennis courts.

"With some of their big shells," said the Captain, "you can hear nothing until it is too late, for the reason that the shell travels more quickly than the sound of it. The sounds reach your ears in inverse order—if you are alive."

A moment later a third shell dropped in the same plot of ground.

And even a mile and a half off, at the other end of the communication trench, when the automobiles emerged from their shelter into the view of the captive balloon, the officers feared for the automobiles, and we fled very swiftly.

We had been to the very front of the front, and it was the most cheerful, confident, high-spirited place I had seen in France, or in England either.

## III Ruins

When you go into Rheims by the Epernay road, the life of the street seems to be proceeding as usual, except that octroi formalities have been abolished. Women, some young and beautiful, stare nonchalantly as the car passes. Children are playing and shrieking in the sunshine; the little cafes and shops keep open door; the baker is busy; middle-aged persons go their ways in meditation upon existence. It is true there are soldiers; but there are soldiers in every important French town at all seasons of the year in peace-time. In short, the spectacle is just that ordinarily presented to the poorer exterior thoroughfares leading towards the centre of a city.

And yet, in two minutes, in less than two minutes, you may be in a quarter where no life is left. This considerable quarter is not seriously damaged—it is destroyed. Not many houses, but every house in it will have to be rebuilt from the cellars. This quarter is desolation. Large shops, large houses, small shops, and small houses have all been treated alike. The facade may stand, the roof may have fallen in entirely or only partially, floors may have disappeared altogether or may still be clinging at odd angles to the walls—the middle of every building is the same: a vast heap of what once was the material of a home or a business, and what now is foul rubbish. In many instances the shells have revealed the functioning of the home at its most intimate, and that is seen which none should see. Indignation rises out of the heart. Amid stacks of refuse you may distinguish a bath, a magnificent fragment of mirror, a piece of tapestry, a saucepan. In a funeral shop wreaths still hang on their hooks for sale. Telephone and telegraph wires depend in a loose tangle from the poles. The clock of the Protestant church has stopped at a quarter to six. The shells have been freakish. In one building a shell harmlessly made a hole in the courtyard large enough to bury every commander of a German army; another shell—a 210 mm.—went through an inner wall and opened up the cellars by destroying 150 square feet of ground-floor: ten people were in the cellars, and none was hurt. Uninjured signs of cafes and shops, such as "The Good Hope," "The Success of the Day," meet your gaze with sardonic calm.

The inhabitants of this quarter, and of other quarters in Rheims, have gone. Some are dead. Others are picnicking in Epernay, Paris, elsewhere. They have left everything behind them, and yet they have left nothing. Each knows his lot in the immense tragedy. Nobody can realise the whole of the tragedy. It defies the mind; and, moreover, the horror of it is allayed somewhat by the beautiful forms which ruin—even the ruin of modern ugly architecture—occasionally takes. The effect of the pallor of a bedroom wall-paper against smoke-blackened masonry, where some corner of a house sticks up like a tall, serrated column out of the confusion, remains obstinately in the memory, symbolising, somehow, the grand German deed.

For do not forget that this quarter accurately represents what the Germans came out of Germany into France deliberately to do. This material devastation, this annihilation of effort, hope, and love, this substitution of sorrow for joy—is just what plans and guns were laid for, what the worshipped leaders of the Fatherland prepared with the most wanton and scientific solicitude. It is desperately cruel. But it is far worse than cruel—it is idiotic in its immense futility. The perfect idiocy of the thing overwhelms you. And to your reason it is monstrous that one population should overrun another with murder and destruction from political covetousness as that two populations should go to war concerning a religious creed. Indeed, it is more monstrous. It is an obscene survival, a phenomenon that has strayed through some negligence of fate, into the wrong century.

Strange, in an adjoining quarter, partly but not utterly destroyed, a man is coming home in a cab with luggage from the station, and the servant-girl waits for him at the house-door. And I heard of a case where a property-owner who had begun to build a house just before the war has lately resumed building operations. In the Esplanade Ceres the fountain is playing amid all the ravage; and the German trenches, in that direction, are not more than two miles away.

It is quite impossible for any sane man to examine the geography of the region of destruction which I have so summarily described without being convinced that the Germans, in shelling it, were simply aiming at the Cathedral. Tracing the streets affected, one can follow distinctly the process of their searching for the precise range of the Cathedral. Practically the whole of the damage is concentrated on the line of the Cathedral.

But the Cathedral stands.

Its parvis is grass-grown; the hotels on the parvis are heavily battered, and if they are not destroyed it is because the Cathedral sheltered them; the Archbishop's palace lies in fragments; all around is complete ruin. But the Cathedral stands, high above the level of disaster, a unique target, and a target successfully defiant. The outer roof is quite gone; much masonry is smashed; some of the calcined statues have exactly the appearance of tortured human flesh. But in its essence, and in its splendid outlines, the building remains—apparently unconquerable. The towers are particularly serene and impressive. The deterioration is, of course, tremendously severe. Scores, if not hundreds, of statues, each of which was a masterpiece, are spoilt; great quantities of carving are defaced; quite half the glass is irremediably broken; the whole of the interior non-structural decoration is destroyed. But the massiveness of the Cathedral has withstood German shrapnel. The place will never be the same again, or nearly the same. Nevertheless, Rheims Cathedral triumphantly exists.

The Germans use it as a vent for their irritation. When things go wrong for them at other parts of the front, they shell Rheims Cathedral. It has absolutely no military interest, but it is beloved by civilised mankind, and therefore is a means of offence. The French tried to remove some of the glass, utilising an old scaffolding. At once the German shells came. Nothing was to be saved that shrapnel could destroy. Shrapnel is futile against the body of the Cathedral, as is proved by the fact that 3,000 shells have fallen on or near it in a day and a night. If the Germans used high-explosive, one might believe that they had some deep religious aim necessitating the non-existence of the Cathedral. But they do not use high-explosive here. Shrapnel merely and uselessly torments.

When I first saw the Cathedral I was told that there had been calm for several days. I know that German agents in neutral countries constantly deny that the Cathedral is now shelled. When I saw the Cathedral again the next morning, five shells had just been aimed at it. I inspected the hole excavated by a 155-mm. shell at the foot of the eastern extremity, close to the walls. This hole was certainly not there when I made the circuit of the Cathedral on the previous evening. It came into existence at 6.40 a.m., and I inspected it at 8.20 a.m., and a newspaper boy offered me that morning's paper on the very edge of it. A fragment of shell, picked up warm by the architect in charge of the Cathedral and given to me, is now in my pocket.

We had a luncheon party at Rheims, in a certain hotel. This hotel had been closed for a time, but the landlady had taken heart again. The personnel appeared to consist solely of the landlady and a relative. Both women were in mourning. They served us themselves, and the meal was excellent, though one could get neither soda-water nor cigars. Shells had greeted the city a few hours earlier, but their effect had been only material; they are entirely ignored by the steadfast inhabitants, who do their primitive business in the desolated, paralysed organism with an indifference which is as resigned as it is stoic. Those ladies might well have been blown to bits as they crossed the courtyard bearing a dish of cherries or a bottle of wine. The sun shone steadily on the rich foliage of the street, and dogs and children rollicked mildly beneath the branches. Several officers were with us, including two Staff officers. These officers, not belonging to the same unit, had a great deal to tell each other and us: so much, that the luncheon lasted nearly two hours. Some of them had been in the retreat, in the battles of the Marne and of the Aisne, and in the subsequent trench fighting; none had got a scratch. Of an unsurpassed urbanity and austerity themselves, forming part of the finest civilisation which this world has yet seen, thoroughly appreciative of the subtle and powerful qualities of the race to which they belong, they exhibited a chill and restrained surprise at the manners of the invaders. One had seen two thousand champagne bottles strewn around a chateau from which the invaders had decamped, and the old butler of the house going carefully through the grounds and picking up the bottles which by chance had not been opened. The method of opening champagne, by the way, was a stroke of the sabre on the neck of the bottle. The German manner was also to lay the lighted cigar on the finest table-linen, so that by the burnt holes the proprietors might count their guests. Another officer had seen a whole countryside of villages littered with orchestrions and absinthe- bottles, groundwork of an interrupted musical and bacchic fete whose details must be imagined, like many other revolting and scabrous details, which no compositor would consent to set up in type, but which, nevertheless, are known and form a striking part of the unwritten history of the attack on civilisation. You may have read hints of these things again and again, but no amount of previous preparation will soften for you the shock of getting them first-hand from eyewitnesses whose absolute reliability it would be fatuous to question.

What these men with their vivid gestures, bright eyes, and perfect phrasing most delight in is personal heroism. And be it remembered that, though they do tell a funny story about German scouts who, in order to do their work, painted themselves the green of trees—and then, to complete the illusion, when they saw a Frenchman began to tremble like leaves—they give full value to the courage of the invaders. But, of course, it is the courage of Frenchmen that inspires their narrations. I was ever so faintly surprised by their candid and enthusiastic appreciation of the heroism of the auxiliary services. They were lyrical about engine-drivers, telephone- repairers, stretcher-bearers, and so on. The story which had the most success concerned a soldier (a schoolmaster) who in an engagement got left between the opposing lines, a quite defenceless mark for German rifles. When a bullet hit him, he cried, "Vive la France!"

When he was missed he kept silent. He was hit again and again, and at each wound he cried, "Vive la France!" He could not be killed. At last they turned a machine-gun on him and raked him from head to foot. "Vive la———"

It was a long, windy, dusty drive to Arras. The straight, worn roads of flinty chalk passed for many miles ARRAS through country where there was no unmilitary activity save that of the crops pushing themselves up. Everything was dedicated to the war. Only at one dirty little industrial town did we see a large crowd of men waiting after lunch to go into a factory. These male civilians had a very odd appearance; it was as though they had been left out of the war by accident, or by some surprising benevolence. One thought first, "There must be some mistake here." But there was probably no mistake. These men were doubtless in the immense machine.

After we had traversed a more attractive agricultural town, with a town hall whose architecture showed that Flanders was not very far off, the soil changed and the country grew more sylvan and delectable. And the sun shone hotly. Camps alternated with orchards, and cows roamed in the camps and also in the orchards. And among the trees could be seen the blue draperies of women at work. Then the wires of the field-telephones and telegraphs on their elegantly slim bamboos were running alongside us. And once or twice, roughly painted on a bit of bare wood, we saw the sign: "Vers le Front." Why any sign should be necessary for such a destination I could not imagine. But perhaps humour had entered into the matter. At length we perceived Arras in the distance, and at a few kilometres it looked rather like itself: it might have been a living city.

When, however, you actually reach Arras you cannot be deceived for an instant as to what has happened to the place. It offers none of the transient illusion of Rheims. The first street you see is a desolation, empty and sinister. Grimy curtains bulge out at smashed windows. Everywhere the damage of shells is visible. The roadway and the pavements are littered with bits of homes. Grass flourishes among the bits. You proceed a little further to a large, circular place, once imposing. Every house in it presents the same blighted aspect. There is no urban stir. But in the brief intervals of the deafening cannonade can be heard one sound—blinds and curtains fluttering against empty window-frames and perhaps the idle, faint banging of a loose shutter. Not even a cat walks. We are alone, we and the small group of Staff officers who are acting as our hosts. We feel like thieves, like desecrators, impiously prying. At the other side of the place a shell has dropped before a house and sliced away all its front. On the ground floor is the drawing-room. Above that is the bedroom, with the bed made and the white linen smoothly showing. The marvel is that the bed, with all the other furniture, does not slide down the sloping floor into the street. But everything remains moveless and placid. The bedroom is like a show. It might be the bedroom of some famous man exposed to worshipping tourists at sixpence a head. A few chairs have fallen out of the house, and they lie topsy-turvy in the street amid the debris; no one has thought to touch them. In all directions thoroughfares branch forth, silent, grass-grown, and ruined.

"You see the strong fortress I have!" says the Commanding Officer with genial sarcasm. "You notice its high military value. It is open at every end. You can walk into it as easily as into a windmill. And yet they bombard it. Yesterday they fired twenty projectiles a minute for an hour into the town.

A performance absolutely useless! Simple destruction! But they are like that!"

So we went forward further into the city, and saw sights still stranger. Of one house nothing but the roof was left, the roof made a triumphal arch. Everywhere potted plants, boxed against walls or suspended from window-frames, were freshly blooming. All the streets were covered with powdered glass. In many streets telegraph and telephone wires hung in thick festoons like abandoned webs of spiders, or curled themselves round the feet; continually one had to be extricating oneself from them. Continually came the hollow sound of things falling and slipping within the smashed interiors behind the facades. And then came the sound of a baby crying. For this city is not, after all, uninhabited. We saw a woman coming out of her house and carefully locking the door behind her. Was she locking it against shells, or against burglars? Observe those pipes rising through gratings in the pavement, and blue smoke issuing therefrom. Those pipes are the outward sign that such inhabitants as remain have transformed their cellars into drawing-rooms and bedrooms. We descended into one such home. The real drawing-room, on the ground-floor, had been invaded by a shell. In that apartment richly-carved furniture was mixed up with pieces of wall and pieces of curtain under a thick layer of white dust. But this underground home, with its arched roof and aspect of extreme solidity, was tidy and very snugly complete in all its arrangements, and the dark entrance to it well protected against the hazards of bombardment.

"Nevertheless," said the master of the home, "a 210-mm. shell would penetrate everything. It would be the end."

He threw up his hands with a nonchalant gesture. He was a fatalist worthy of his city, which is now being besieged and ruined not for the first time. The Vandals (I mean the original Vandals) laid waste Arras again and again. Then the Franks took it. Then, in the ninth century, the Normans ravaged it; and then Charles the Simple; and then Lothair; and then Hugh Capet. In the fifteenth century Charles VI. besieged it for seven weeks, and did not take it. Under Louis XI. it was atrociously outraged. It revolted, and was retaken by assault, its walls razed, its citizens expatriated, and its name changed.

Useless! The name returned, and the citizens. At the end of the fifteenth century it fell under Spanish rule, and had no kind of peace whatever until after another siege by a large French army, it was regained by France in 1640. Fourteen years later the House of Austria had yet another try for it, and the Archduke Leopold laid siege to the city. He lost 7,000 men, 64 guns, 3,000 horses, and all his transport, and fled. (Last August was the first August in two hundred and sixty years which has not witnessed a municipal fete in celebration of this affair.) Since then Arras has had a tolerably quiet time, except during the Revolution. It suffered nothing in 1870. It now suffers. And apparently those inhabitants who have stood fast have not forgotten how to suffer; history must be in their veins.

In the street where we first noticed the stove-pipes sprouting from the pavement, we saw a postman in the regulation costume of the French postman, with the regulation black, shiny wallet-box hanging over his stomach, and the regulation pen behind his ear, smartly delivering letters from house to house. He did not knock at the doors; he just stuck the letters through the empty window-frames. He was a truly remarkable sight.

Then we arrived by a curved street at the Cathedral of St. Vaast. St. Vaast, who preached Christianity after it had been forgotten in Arras, is all over the district in the nomenclature of places. Nobody among the dilettanti has a good word to say for the Cathedral, which was built in the latter half of the eighteenth and the first half of the nineteenth centuries, and which exhibits a kind of simple baroque style, with Corinthian pillars in two storeys. But Arras Cathedral is the most majestic and striking ruin at the Front. It is superlatively well placed on an eminence by itself, and its dimensions are tremendous. It towers over the city far more imposingly than Chartres Cathedral towers over Chartres. The pale simplicity of its enormous lines and surfaces renders it better suited for the martyrdom of bombardment than any Gothic building could possibly be. The wounds are clearly visible on its flat facades, uncomplicated by much carving and statuary. They are terrible wounds, yet they do not appreciably impair the ensemble of the fane. Photographs and pictures of Arras Cathedral ought to be cherished by German commanders, for they have accomplished nothing more austerely picturesque, more religiously impressive, more idiotically sacrilegious, more exquisitely futile than their achievement here. And they are adding to it weekly. As a spectacle, the Cathedral of Rheims cannot compare with the Cathedral of Arras.

In the north transept a 325-mm. shell has knocked a clean hole through which a mastodon might wriggle. Just opposite this transept, amid universal wreckage, a cafe is miraculously preserved. Its glass, mugs, counters, chairs, and ornaments are all there, covered with white dust, exactly as they were left one night. You could put your hand through a window aperture and pick up a glass. Close by, the lovely rafter-work of an old house is exposed, and, within, a beam has fallen from the roof to the ground. This beam is burning. The flames are industriously eating away at it, like a tiger gnawing in tranquil content at its prey which it has dragged to a place of concealment. There are other fires in Arras, and have been for some days. But what are you to do? A step further on is a greengrocer's shop, open and doing business.

We gradually circled round the Cathedral until we arrived at the Town Hall, built in the sixteenth century, very carefully restored in the nineteenth, and knocked to pieces in the twentieth. We approached it from the back, and could not immediately perceive what had happened to it, for later erections have clustered round it, and some of these still existed in their main outlines. In a great courtyard stood an automobile, which certainly had not moved for months. It was a wreck, overgrown with rust and pustules. This automobile well symbolised the desolation, open and concealed, by which it was surrounded. A touchingly forlorn thing, dead and deaf to the never-ceasing, ever-reverberating chorus of the guns!

To the right of the Town Hall, looking at it from the rear, we saw a curving double row of mounds of brick, stone, and refuse. Understand: these had no resemblance to houses; they had no resemblance to anything whatever except mounds of brick, stone, and refuse. The sight of them acutely tickled my curiosity. "What is this?"

"It is the principal street in Arras." The mind could picture it at once— one of those narrow, winding streets which in ancient cities perpetuate the most ancient habits of the citizens, maintaining their commercial pre-eminence in the face of all town-planning; a street leading to the Town Hall; a dark street full of jewellers' shops and ornamented women and correctness and the triumph of correctness; a street of the "best" shops, of high rents, of famous names, of picturesque signs; a street where the wheels of traffic were continually interlocking, but a street which would not, under any consideration, have widened itself by a single foot, because its narrowness was part of its prestige. Well, German gunnery has brought that street to an end past all resuscitation. It may be rebuilt— it will never be the same street.

"What's the name of the street?" I asked.

None of the officers in the party could recall the name of the principal business street in Arras, and there was no citizen within hail. The very name had gone, like the forms of the houses. I have since searched for it in guides, encyclopaedias, and plans; but it has escaped me withdrawn and lost, for me, in the depths of history.

The street had suffered, not at all on its own account, but because it happened to be in the line of fire of the Town Hall. It merely received some portion of the blessings which were intended for the Town Hall, but which overshot their mark. The Town Hall (like the Cathedrals here and at Rheims) had no military interest or value, but it was the finest thing in Arras, the most loved thing, an irreplaceable thing; and therefore the Germans made a set at it, as they made a set at the Cathedrals. It is just as if, having got an aim on a soldier's baby, they had started to pick off its hands and feet, saying to the soldier: "Yield, or we will finish your baby." Either the military ratiocination is thus, or the deed is simple lunacy.

When we had walked round to the front of the Town Hall we were able to judge to what extent the beautiful building had monopolised the interest of the Germans. The Town Hall stands at the head of a magnificent and enormous arcaded square, uniform in architecture, and no doubt dating from the Spanish occupation. Seeing this square, and its scarcely smaller sister a little further on, you realise that indeed you are in a noble city. The square had hardly been touched by the bombardment. There had been no shells to waste on the square while the more precious Town Hall had one stone left upon another. From the lower end of the square, sheltered from the rain by the arcade, I made a rough sketch of what remains of the Town Hall. Comparing this sketch with an engraved view taken from exactly the same spot, one can see graphically what had occurred. A few arches of the ground-floor colonnade had survived in outline. Of the upper part of the facade nothing was left save a fragment of wall showing two window-holes. The rest of the facade, and the whole of the roof, was abolished. The later building attached to the left of the facade had completely disappeared. The carved masonry of the earlier building to the right of the facade had survived in a state of severe mutilation. The belfry which, rising immediately behind the Town Hall, was once the highest belfry in France (nearly 250 feet), had vanished. The stump of it, jagged like the stump of a broken tooth, obstinately persisted, sticking itself up to a level a few feet higher than the former level of the crest of the roof. The vast ruin was heaped about with refuse.

Arras is not in Germany. It is in France. I mention this fact because it is notorious that Germany is engaged in a defensive war, and in a war for the upholding of the highest civilisation. The Germans came all the way across Belgium, and thus far into France, in order to defend themselves against attack. They defaced and destroyed all the beauties of Arras, and transformed it into a scene of desolation unsurpassed in France, so that the highest civilisation might remain secure and their own hearths intact. One wonders what the Germans would have done had they been fighting, not a war of defence and civilisation, but a war of conquest and barbarism. The conjecture may, perhaps, legitimately occupy the brains of citizens. In any case, the French Government would do well to invite to such places as Arras, Soissons, and Senlis groups of Mayors of the cities of all countries, so that these august magistrates may behold for themselves and realise in their souls what defensive war and the highest civilisation actually do mean when they come to the point.

Personally, I am against a policy of reprisals, and yet I do not see how Germany can truly appreciate what she has done unless an object-lesson is created for her out of one of her own cities. And she emphatically ought to appreciate what she has done. One city would suffice. If, at the end of the war, Cologne were left as Arras was when I visited it, a definite process of education would have been accomplished in the Teutonic mind. The event would be hard on Cologne, but not harder than the other event has been on Arras. Moreover, it is held, I believe, that the misfortunes of war bring out all that is finest in the character of a nation, and that therefore war, with its sweet accompaniments, is a good and a necessary thing. I am against a policy of reprisals, and yet—such is human nature— having seen Arras, I would honestly give a year's income to see Cologne in the same condition. And to the end of my life I shall feel cheated if Cologne or some similar German town is not in fact ultimately reduced to the same condition. This state of mind comes of seeing things with your own eyes.

Proceeding, we walked through a mile or two of streets in which not one house was inhabited nor undamaged. Some of these streets had been swept, so that at the first glance they seemed to be streets where all the citizens were indoors, reflecting behind drawn blinds and closed shutters upon some incredible happening. But there was nobody indoors. There was nobody in the whole quarter— only ourselves; and we were very unhappy and unquiet in the solitude. Almost every window was broken; every wall was chipped; chunks had been knocked out of walls, and at intervals there was no wall. One house showed the different paperings of six rooms all completely exposed to the gaze. The proprietor evidently had a passion for anthracite stoves; in each of the six fireplaces was an anthracite stove, and none had fallen. The post office was shattered.

Then the railway station of Arras! A comparatively new railway station, built by the Compagnie du Nord in 1898. A rather impressive railway station. The great paved place in front of it was pitted with shell-holes of various sizes. A shell had just grazed the elaborate facade, shaving ornaments and mouldings off it. Every pane of glass in it was smashed. All the ironwork had a rich brown rust. The indications for passengers were plainly visible. Here you must take your ticket; here you must register your baggage; here you must wait. We could look through the station as through the ribs of a skeleton. The stillness of it under the rain and under the echoes of the tireless artillery was horrible. It was the most unnatural, ghostly, ghastly railway station one could imagine. As within the station, so on the platforms. All the glass of the shelters for passengers was broken to little bits; the ironwork thickly encrusted. The signals were unutterably forlorn in their ruin. And on the lines themselves rampant vegetation had grown four feet high—a conquering jungle. The defence of German soil is a mighty and a far-reaching affair. This was on July 7th, 1915.

## IV At Grips

I have before referred to the apparent vagueness and casualness of war on its present scarcely conceivable scale. When you are with a Staff officer, you see almost everything. I doubt not that certain matters are hidden from you; but, broadly speaking, you do see all that is to be seen. Into the mind of the General, which conceals the strategy that is to make history, of course you cannot peer. The General is full of interesting talk about the past and about the present, but about the future he breathes no word. If he is near the centre of the front he will tell you blandly, in answer to your question, that a great movement may not improbably be expected at the wings. If he is at either of the wings he will tell you blandly that a great movement may not improbably be expected at the centre. You are not disappointed at his attitude, because you feel when putting them that such questions as yours deserve such answers as his. But you are assuredly disappointed at not being able to comprehend even the present—what is going on around you, under your eyes, deafening your ears.

For example, I hear the sound of guns. I do not mean the general sound of guns, which is practically continuous round the horizon, but the particular sound of some specific group of guns. I ask about them. Sometimes even Staff officers may hesitate before deciding whether they are enemy guns or French guns. As a rule, the civilian distinguishes an enemy shot by the sizzling, affrighting sound of the projectile as it rushes through the air towards him; whereas the French projectile, rushing away from him, is out of hearing before the noise of the gun's explosion has left his ears. But I may be almost equidistant between a group of German and a group of French guns.

When I have learnt what the guns are and their calibre, and, perhaps, even their approximate situation on the large-scale Staff map, I am not much nearer the realisation of them. Actually to find them might be half a day's work, and when I have found them I have simply found several pieces of mechanism each hidden in a kind of hut, functioning quite privately and disconnectedly by the aid of a few perspiring men. The affair is not like shooting at anything. A polished missile is shoved into the gun. A horrid bang—the missile has disappeared, has simply gone. Where it has gone, what it has done, nobody in the hut seems to care. There is a telephone close by, but only numbers and formulae—and perhaps an occasional rebuke—come out of the telephone, in response to which the perspiring men make minute adjustments in the gun or in the next missile.

Of the target I am absolutely ignorant, and so are the perspiring men. I am free to go forth and look for the target. It is pointed out to me. It may be a building or a group of buildings; it may be something else. At best, it is nothing but a distant spot on a highly complex countryside. I see a faint puff of smoke, seemingly as harmless as a feather momentarily floating. And I think: Can any reasonable person expect that those men with that noisy contrivance in the enclosed hut away back shall plant a mass of metal into that far-off tiny red patch of masonry lost in the vast landscape? And, even if by chance they do, for what reason has that particular patch been selected? What influence could its destruction have on the mighty course of the struggle? . . . Thus it is that war seems vague and casual, because a mere fragment of it defeats the imagination, and the bits of even the fragment cannot be fitted together. Why, I have stood in the first-line trench itself and heard a fusillade all round me, and yet have seen nothing and understood nothing of the action!

It is the same with the movements of troops. For example, I slept in a town behind the front, IN and I was wakened up—not, as often, by an aeroplane—but by a tremendous shaking and throbbing of the hotel. This went on for a long time, from just after dawn till about six o'clock, when it stopped, only to recommence after a few minutes. I got up, and found that, in addition to the hotel, the whole town was shaking and throbbing. A regiment was passing through it in auto- buses. Each auto-bus held about thirty men, and the vehicles rattled after one another at a distance of at most thirty yards. The auto- buses were painted the colour of battleships, and were absolutely uniform except that some had permanent and some only temporary roofs, and some had mica windows and some only holes in the sides. All carried the same number of soldiers, and in all the rifles were stacked in precisely the same fashion. When one auto-bus stopped, all stopped, and the soldiers waved and smiled to girls at windows and in the street. The entire town had begun its day. No matter how early you arise in these towns, the town has always begun its day.

The soldiers in their pale-blue uniforms were young, lively, high- spirited, and very dusty; their moustaches, hair, and ears were noticeably coated with dust. Evidently they had been travelling for hours. The auto-buses kept appearing out of the sun-shot dust- cloud at the end of the town, and disappearing round the curve by the Town Hall. Occasionally an officer's automobile, or a car with a couple of nurses, would intervene momentarily; and then more and more and more auto-buses, and still more. The impression given is that the entire French Army is passing through the town. The rattle and the throbbing and the shaking get on my nerves. At last come two breakdown-vans, and the procession is finished. I cannot believe that it is really finished, but it is; and the silence is incredible.

Well, I have seen only a couple of regiments go by. Out of the hundreds of regiments in the French Army, just two! But whence they had come, what they had done, whither they were travelling, what they were intended to do—nobody could tell me. They had an air as casual and vague and aimless as a flight of birds across a landscape.

There were more picturesque pilgrimages than that. One of the most picturesque and touching spectacles I saw at the front was the march of a regiment of the line into another little country town on a very fine summer morning. First came the regimental band. The brass instruments were tarnished; the musicians had all sorts of paper packages tied to their knapsacks. Besides being musicians they were real soldiers, in war-stained uniforms. They marched with an air of fatigue. But the tune they played was bright enough. Followed some cyclists, keeping pace with the marchers. Then an officer on a horse. Then companies of the regiment. The stocks of many of the rifles were wrapped in dirty rags. Every man carried all that was his in the campaign, including a pair of field-glasses. Every man was piled up with impedimenta—broken, torn, soiled and cobbled impedimenta. And every man was very, very tired.

A young officer on foot could scarcely walk. He moved in a kind of trance, and each step was difficult. He may have been half asleep. At intervals a triangular sign was borne aloft—red, blue, or some other tint. These signs indicated the positions of the different companies in the trenches. (Needless to say that the regiment had come during the night from a long spell of the trenches—but what trenches?) Then came the gorgeous regimental colours, and every soldier in the street saluted them, and every civilian raised his hat.

I noticed more and more that the men were exhausted, were at the limit of their endurance. Then passed a group which was quite fresh. A Red Cross detachment! No doubt they had had very little to do. After them a few horses, grey and white; and then field-kitchens and equipment-carts. And then a machine-gun on a horse's back; others in carts; pack-mules with ammunition-boxes; several more machine-gun sections. And then more field-kitchens. In one of these the next meal was actually preparing, and steam rose from under a great iron lid. On every cart was a spare wheel for emergencies; the hub of every wheel was plaited round with straw; the harness was partly of leather and partly of rope ending in iron hooks. Later came a long Red Cross van, and after it another field-kitchen encumbered with bags and raw meat and strange oddments, and through the interstices of the pile, creeping among bags and raw meat, steam gently mounted, for a meal was maturing in that perambulating kitchen also. Lastly, came a cart full of stretchers and field-hospital apparatus. The regiment, its music still faintly audible, had gone by—self-contained, self-supporting. There was no showiness of a review, but the normal functioning, the actual dailiness, of a line regiment as it lives strenuously in the midst of war.

My desire was that the young officer in a trance should find a good bed instantly. The whole thing was fine; it was pathetic; and, above all, it was mysterious. What was the part of that regiment in the gigantic tactics of Joffre?

However, after a short experience at the front one realises that though the conduct of the campaign may be mysterious, it is neither vague nor casual. I remember penetrating through a large factory into a small village which constituted one of the latest French conquests. An officer who had seen the spot just after it was taken, and before it was "organised," described to me the appearance of the men with their sunken eyes and blackened skins on the day of victory. They were all very cheerful when I saw them; but how alert, how apprehensive, how watchful! I felt that I was in a place where anything might happen at any moment. The village and the factory were a maze of trenches, redoubts, caves, stairs up and stairs down, machine-guns, barbed wire, enfilading devices were all ready. When we climbed to an attic-floor to look at the German positions, which were not fifty yards away, the Commandant was in a fever till we came down again, lest the Germans might spy us and shell his soldiers. He did not so much mind them shelling us, but he objected to them shelling his men. We came down the damaged stairs in safety.

A way had been knocked longitudinally through a whole row of cottages. We went along this—it was a lane of watchful figures—and then it was whispered to us not to talk, for the Germans might hear! And we peered into mines and burrowed and crawled. We disappeared into long subterranean passages and emerged among a lot of soldiers gaily eating as they stood. Close by were a group of men practising with hand-grenades made harmless for the occasion. I followed the Commandant round a corner, and we gazed at I forget what. "Don't stay here," said the Commandant. I moved away. A second after I had moved a bullet struck the wall where I had been standing. The entire atmosphere of the place, with its imminent sense of danger from an invisible enemy and fierce expectation of damaging that enemy, brought home to me the grand essential truth of the front, namely, that the antagonists are continually at grips, like wrestlers, and straining every muscle to obtain the slightest advantage. "Casual" would be the very last adjective to apply to those activities.

Once, after a roundabout tour on foot, one of the Staff Captains ordered an automobile to meet us at the end of a certain road. Part of this road was exposed to German artillery four or five miles off. No sooner had the car come down the road than we heard the fearsome sizzling of an approaching shell. We saw the shell burst before the sound of the sizzling had ceased. Then came the roar of the explosion. The shell was a 77-mm. high-explosive. It fell out of nowhere on the road. The German artillery methodically searched the exposed portion of the road for about half an hour. The shells dropped on it or close by it at intervals of two minutes, and they were planted at even distances of about a hundred yards up and down the slope. I watched the operation from a dug-out close by. It was an exact and a rather terrifying operation. It showed that the invisible Germans were letting nothing whatever go by; but it did seem to me to be a fine waste of ammunition, and a very stupid application of a scientific ideal; for while shelling it the Germans must have noticed that there was nothing at all on the road. We naturally decided not to go up that road in the car, but to skulk through a wood and meet the car in a place of safety. The car had, sooner or later, to go up the road, because there was not another road. The Commandant who was with us was a very seasoned officer, and he regarded all military duties as absolute duties. The car must return along that road. Therefore, let it go. The fact that it was a car serving solely for the convenience of civilians did not influence him. It was a military car, driven by a soldier.

"You may as well go at once," he said to the chauffeur. "We will assist at your agony. What do you say?" he laughingly questioned a subordinate.

"Ah! My Commandant," said the junior officer cautiously, "when it is a question of the service———"

We should naturally have protested against the chauffeur adventuring upon the shell-swept road for our convenience; but he was diplomatic enough to postpone the journey. After a time the shelling ceased, and he passed in safety. He told us when we met him later for the drive home that there were five large holes in the road.

On another occasion, when we were tramping through interminable communication-trenches on a slope, a single rash exposure of two of our figures above the parapet of the trench drew down upon us a bombardment of high-explosive. For myself, I was completely exhausted by the excursion, which was nearing its end, and also I was faint from hunger. But immediately the horrible sizzling sound overhead and an explosion just in front made it plain to me that we were to suffer for a moment's indiscretion, I felt neither fatigue nor hunger. The searching shells fell nearer to us. We ran in couples, with a fair distance between each couple, according to instructions, along the rough, sinuous inequalities of the deep trench. After each visitation we had to lie still and count five till all the fragments of shell had come to rest. At last a shell seemed to drop right upon me. The earth shook under me. My eyes and nose were affected by the fumes of the explosion. But the shell had not dropped right upon me. It had dropped a few yards to the left. A trench is a wonderful contrivance. Immediately afterwards, a friend picked up in the trench one of the warm shots of the charge. It was a many-facetted ball, beautifully made, and calculated to produce the maximum wound. This was the last shell to fall. We were safe. But we realised once again, and more profoundly, that there is nothing casual in the conduct of war.

At no place was the continuously intense character of the struggle— like that of two leviathan wrestlers ever straining their hardest at grips—more effectually brought home to me than in the region known now familiarly to the whole world as Notre Dame de Lorette, from the little chapel that stood on one part of it. An exceedingly ugly little chapel it was, according to the picture postcards. There are thousands of widows and orphans wearing black and regretting the past and trembling about the future to-day simply because the invaders had to be made to give up that religious edifice which they had turned to other uses.

The high, thickly wooded land behind the front was very elaborately organised for living either above ground or underground, according to the circumstances of the day. To describe the organisation would be impolitic. But it included every dodge. And the stores, entombed in safety, comprised all things. I remember, for example, stacks of hundreds of lamp-chimneys. Naught lacked to the completeness of the scene of war. There were even prisoners. I saw two young Germans under guard in a cabin. They said that they had got lost in the labyrinth of trenches, and taken a wrong turning. And I believe they had. One was a Red Cross man—probably a medical student before, with wine and song and boastings, he joined his Gott, his Kaiser, and his comrades in the great mission of civilisation across Belgium. He was dusty and tired, and he looked gloomily at the earthen floor of the cabin. Nevertheless, he had a good carriage and a passably intelligent face, and he was rather handsome. I sympathised with this youth, and I do not think that he was glad to be a prisoner. Some people can go and stare at prisoners, and wreak an idle curiosity upon them. I cannot. A glance, rather surreptitious, and I must walk away. Their humiliation humiliates me, even be they Prussians of the most offensive variety.

A little later we saw another prisoner being brought in—a miserable, tuberculous youth with a nervous trick of the face, thin, very dirty, enfeebled, worn out; his uniform torn, stained, bullet-pierced, and threadbare. Somebody had given him a large hunk of bread, which he had put within the lining of his tunic, it bulged out in front like a paunch. An officer stopped to question him, and while the cross-examination was proceeding a curio-hunting soldier came up behind and cut a button off the tunic. We learnt that the lad was twenty-one years of age, and that he had been called up in December 1914. Before assisting in the conquest of France he was employed in a paper factory. He tried to exhibit gloom, but it was impossible for him quite to conceal his satisfaction in the fact that for him the fighting was over. The wretched boy had had just about enough of world-dominion, and he was ready to let the Hohenzollerns and Junkers finish up the enterprise as best they could without his aid. No doubt, some woman was his mother. It appeared to me that he could not live long, and that the woman in question might never see him again. But every ideal must have its victims; and bereavement, which counts chief among the well-known advantageous moral disciplines of war, is, of course, good for a woman's soul. Besides, that woman would be convinced that her son died gloriously in defence of an attacked Fatherland.

When we had got clear of prisoners and of the innumerable minor tools of war, we came to something essential—namely, a map. This map, which was shown to us rather casually in the middle of a wood, was a very big map, and by means of different coloured chalks it displayed the ground taken from the Germans month by month. The yellow line showed the advance up to May; the blue line showed the further advance up to June; and fresh marks in red showed graphically a further wresting which had occurred only in the previous night. The blue line was like the mark of a tide on a chart; in certain places it had nearly surrounded a German position, and shortly the Germans would have to retire from that position or be cut off. Famous names abounded on that map—such as Souchez, Ablain St. Nazaire, St. Eloi, Fonds de Buval. Being on a very large scale, the map covered a comparatively small section of the front; but, so far as it went, it was a map to be gazed upon with legitimate pride.

The officers regarded it proudly. Eagerly they indicated where the main pressures were, and where new pressures would come later. Their very muscles seemed to be strained in the ardour of their terrific intention to push out and destroy the invader. While admitting, as all the officers I met admitted, the great military qualities of the enemy, they held towards him a more definitely contemptuous attitude than I could discover elsewhere. "When the Boches attack us," said one of them, "we drive them back to their trench, and we take that trench. Thus we advance." But, for them, there was Boche and Boche. It was the Bavarians whom they most respected. They deemed the Prussians markedly inferior as fighters to the Bavarians. The Prussians would not hold firm when seriously menaced. The Prussians, in a word, would not "stick it." Such was the unanimous verdict here.

Out beyond the wood, on the hillside, in the communication- trenches and other trenches, we were enabled to comprehend the true significance of that phrase uttered so carelessly by newspaper- readers—Notre Dame de Lorette. The whole of the ground was in heaps. There was no spot, literally, on which a shell had not burst. Vegetation was quite at an end. The shells seemed to have sterilised the earth. There was not a tree, not a bush, not a blade of any sort, not a root. Even the rankest weeds refused to sprout in the perfect desolation. And this was the incomparable soil of France. The trenches meandered for miles through the pitted brown slopes, and nothing could be seen from them but vast encumbrances of barbed wire. Knotted metal heaped on the unyielding earth!

The solitude of the communication-trenches was appalling, and the continuous roar of the French seventy-fives over our heads did not alleviate it. In the other trenches, however, was much humanity, some of it sleeping in deep, obscure retreats, but most of it acutely alive and interested in everything. A Captain with a shabby uniform and a strong Southern accent told us how on March 9th he and his men defended their trench in water up to the waist and lumps of ice in it knocking against their bodies.

"I was summoned to surrender," he laughed. "I did not surrender. We had twenty killed and twenty-four with frostbitten feet as a result of that affair. Yes—March 9th."

March 9th, 1915, obviously divided that officer's life into two parts, and not unnaturally!

A little further on we might hear an officer speaking somewhat ardently into a telephone:

"What are they doing with that gun? They are shooting all over the shop. Tell them exactly———"

Still a little further on, and another officer would lead us to a spot where we could get glimpses of the plain. What a plain! Pit-heads, superb vegetation, and ruined villages—tragic villages illustrating the glories and the transcendent common-sense of war and invasion. That place over there is Souchez—familiar in all mouths from Arkansas to Moscow for six months past. What an object! Look at St. Eloi! Look at Angres! Look at Neuville St. Vaast! And look at Ablain St. Nazaire, the nearest of all! The village of Ablain St. Nazaire seems to consist now chiefly of exposed and blackened rafters; what is left of the church sticks up precisely like a little bleached bone. A vision horrible and incredible in the immense luxuriance of the plain! The French have got Ablain St. Nazaire. We may go to Ablain St. Nazaire ourselves if we will accept the risks of shelling. Soldiers were seriously wounded there on that very day, for we saw them being carried therefrom on stretchers towards the motor-ambulance and the hospital.

After more walking of a very circuitous nature, I noticed a few bricks in the monotonous expanse of dwarf earth-mounds made by shells.

"Hello!" I said. "Was there a cottage here?"

No! What I had discovered was the illustrious chapel of Notre Dame de Lorette.

Then we were in a German trench which the French had taken and transformed into one of their own trenches by turning its face. It had a more massive air than the average French trench, and its cellarage, if I may use this civilian word, was deeper than that of any French trench. The officers said that often a German trench was taken before the men resting in those profound sleeping-holes could get to the surface, and that therefore they only emerged in order to be killed or captured.

After more heavy trudging we came to trenches abandoned by the Germans and not employed by the French, as the front had moved far beyond them. The sides were dilapidated. Old shirts, bits of uniform, ends of straps, damaged field-glass cases, broken rifles, useless grenades lay all about. Here and there was a puddle of greenish water. Millions of flies, many of a sinister bright burnished green, were busily swarming. The forlornness of these trenches was heartrending. It was the most dreadful thing that I saw at the front, surpassing the forlornness of any destroyed village whatsoever. And at intervals in the ghastly residue of war arose a smell unlike any other smell. … A leg could be seen sticking out of the side of the trench. We smelt a number of these smells, and saw a number of these legs. Each leg was a fine leg, well-clad, and superbly shod in almost new boots with nail-protected soles. Each leg was a human leg attached to a human body, and at the other end of the body was presumably a face crushed in the earth. Two strokes with a pick, and the corpses might have been excavated and decently interred. But not one had been touched. Buried in frenzied haste by amateur, imperilled grave-diggers with a military purpose, these dead men decayed at leisure amid the scrap-heap, the cess-pit, the infernal squalor which once had been a neat, clean, scientific German earthwork, and which still earlier had been part of a fair countryside. The French had more urgent jobs on hand than the sepulture of these victims of a caste and an ambition. So they liquefied into corruption in their everlasting boots, proving that there is nothing like leather. They were a symbol. With alacrity we left them to get forward to the alert, straining life of war.

V The British Lines

You should imagine a large plain, but not an empty plain, nor a plain entirely without hills. There are a few hills, including at least one very fine eminence (an agreeable old town on the top), with excellent views of the expanse. The expanse is considerably diversified. In the first place it is very well wooded; in the second place it is very well cultivated; and in the third place it is by no means uninhabited. Villages abound in it; and small market towns are not far off each other. These places are connected by plenty of roads (often paved) and canals, and by quite an average mileage of railways. See the plain from above, and the chief effect is one of trees. The rounded tops of trees everywhere obscure the view, and out of them church-towers stick up; other architecture is only glimpsed. The general tints are green and grey, and the sky as a rule is grey to match. Finally, the difference between Northern France and Southern Belgium is marked only by the language of shop and cafe signs; in most respects the two sections of the Front resemble each other with extraordinary exactitude.

The British occupation—which is marked of course by high and impressive cordiality—is at once superficially striking and subtly profound.

"What do you call your dog?" I asked a ragamuffin who was playing with a nice little terrier in a village street where we ate an at fresco meal of jam-sandwiches with a motor-car for a buffet.

He answered shyly, but with pride:

"Tommy."

The whole countryside is criss-crossed with field telegraph and telephone wires. Still more spectacular, everywhere there are traffic directions. And these directions are very large and very curt. "Motor- lorries dead slow," you see in immense characters in the midst of the foreign scene. And at all the awkward street corners in the towns a soldier directs the traffic. Not merely in the towns, but in many and many a rural road you come across a rival of the Strand. For the traffic is tremendous, and it is almost all mechanical transport. You cannot go far without encountering, not one or two, but dozens and scores of motor-lorries, which, after the leviathan manner of motor-lorries, occupy as much of the road as they can. When a string of these gets mixed up with motor-cars, a few despatch riders on motor cycles, a peasant's cart, and a company on the march, the result easily surpasses Piccadilly Circus just before the curtains are rising in West End theatres. Blocks may and do occur at any moment. Out of a peaceful rustic solitude you may run round a curve straight into a block. The motor-lorries constitute the difficulty, not always because they are a size too large for the country, but sometimes because of the human nature of Tommies. The rule is that on each motor-lorry two Tommies shall ride in front and one behind. The solitary one behind is cut off from mankind, and accordingly his gregarious instinct not infrequently makes him nip on to the front seat in search of companionship. When he is established there impatient traffic in the rear may screech and roar in vain for a pathway; nothing is so deaf as a motor-lorry. The situation has no disadvantage for the trio in front of the motor-lorry until a Staff officer's car happens to be inconvenienced. Then, when the Staff officer does get level, there is a short, sharp scene, a dead silence, and the offender creeps back, a stricken sinner, to his proper post.

The encumbered and busy roads, and the towns crammed with vehicles and vibrating with military activity, produce upon you such an overwhelming impression of a vast and complex organisation that your thought rushes instantly to the supreme controller of that organisation, the man ultimately responsible for all of it. He does not make himself invisible. It becomes known that he will see you at a certain hour. You arrive a few minutes before that hour. The building is spacious, and its Gallic aspect is intensified by the pure Anglo- Saxonism of its terrific inhabitants. In a large outer office you are presented to the various brains of the Expeditionary Force, all members of the General Staff—famous names among them, celebrities, specialists, illustrious with long renown. They walk in and out, and they sit smoking and chatting, as if none of them was anybody in particular. And as a fact, you find it a little difficult to appreciate them at their lawful worth, because you are aware that in the next room, behind those double doors, is he at whose nod the greatest among them tremble.

"The Commander-in-Chief will see you." You go forward, and I defy you not to be daunted.

The inner chamber has been a drawing-room. It still is partially a drawing-room. The silk panels on the walls have remained, and in one corner a grand piano lingers. In the middle is a plain table bearing a map on a huge scale. There he is, the legendary figure. You at last have proof that he exists. He comes towards the door to meet you. A thick-set man, not tall, with small hands and feet, and finger-nails full of character. He has a short white moustache, and very light-coloured eyes set in a ruddy complexion. His chin is noticeable. He is not a bit dandiacal. He speaks quietly and grimly and reflectively. He is a preoccupied man. He walks a little to and fro, pausing between his short, sparse sentences. When he talks of the Germans he has a way of settling his head and neck with a slight defiant shake well between his shoulders. I have seen the gesture in experienced boxers and in men of business when openly or implicitly challenged. It is just as if he had said: "Wait a bit! I shall get even with that lot—and let no one imagine the contrary!" From the personality of the man there emanates all the time a pugnacious and fierce doggedness. After he has formally welcomed you into the meshes of his intimidating organisation, and made a few general observations, he says, in a new tone: "Well———," and you depart. And as you pass out of the building the thought in your mind is:

"I have seen him!" After the Commander-in-Chief there are two other outstanding and separately existing notabilities in connection with the General Staff. One is the Quartermaster-General, who superintends the supply of all material; and the other is the Adjutant-General, who superintends the supply of men. With the latter is that formidable instrument of authority, the Grand Provost Marshal, who superintends behaviour and has the power of life and death. Each of these has his Staff, and each is housed similarly to the Commander-in-Chief. Then each Army (for there is more than one army functioning as a distinct entity)—each Army has its Commander with his Staff. And each Corps of each Army has its Commander with his Staff. And each Division of each Corps of each Army has its Commander with his Staff. And each Brigade of each Division of each Corps of each Army has its Commander with his Staff; but though I met several Brigadier-Generals, I never saw one at his head-quarters with his Staff. I somehow could not penetrate lower than the entity of a Division. I lunched, had tea, and dined at the headquarters of various of these Staffs, with a General as host. They were all admirably housed, and their outward circumstances showed a marked similarity. The most memorable thing about them was their unending industry.

"You have a beautiful garden," I said to one General.

"Yes," he said. "I have never been into it."

He told me that he rose at six and went to bed at midnight.

As soon as coffee is over after dinner, and before cigars are over, the General will say:

"I don't wish to seem inhospitable, but————"

And a few minutes later you may see a large lighted limousine moving off into the night, bearing Staff officers to their offices for the evening seance of work which ends at twelve o'clock or thereabouts.

The complexity and volume of work which goes on at even a Divisional Headquarters, having dominion over about twenty thousand full-grown males, may be imagined; and that the bulk of such work is of a business nature, including much tiresome routine, is certain. Of the strictly military labours of Headquarters, that which most agreeably strikes the civilian is the photography and the map-work. I saw thousands of maps. I inspected thick files of maps all showing the same square of country under different military conditions at different dates. And I learnt that special maps are regularly circulated among all field officers.

The fitting-out and repairing sheds of the Royal Flying Corps were superb and complete constructions, at once practical and very elegant. I visited them in the midst of a storm. The equipment was prodigious; the output was prodigious; the organisation was scientific; and the staff was both congenial and impressive. When one sees these birdcages full of birds and comprehends the spirit of flight, one is less surprised at the unimaginable feats which are daily performed over there in the sky northwards and eastwards. I saw a man who flew over Ghent twice a week with the regularity of a train. He had never been seriously hit. These airmen have a curious physical advantage. The noise of their own engine, it is said, prevents them from hearing the explosions of the shrapnel aimed at them.

The British soldier in France and Flanders is not a self-supporting body.

He needs support, and a great deal of support. I once saw his day's rations set forth on a tray, and it seemed to me that I could not have consumed them in a week of good appetite. The round of meat is flanked by plenteous bacon, jam, cheese, and bread. In addition there are vegetables, tea, sugar, salt, and condiments, with occasional butter; and once a week come two ounces of tobacco and a box of matches for each ounce. But the formidable item is the meat. And then the British soldier wants more than food; he wants, for instance, fuel, letters, cleanliness; he wants clothing, and all the innumerable instruments and implements of war. He wants regularly, and all the time.

Hence you have to imagine wide steady streams of all manner of things converging upon Northern France not only from Britain but from round about the globe. The force of an imperative demand draws them powerfully in, night and day, as a magnet might. It is impossible to trace exactly either the direction or the separate constituents of these great streams of necessaries. But it is possible to catch them, or at any rate one of them, at the most interesting point of its course: the point at which the stream, made up of many converging streams, divides suddenly and becomes many streams again.

That point is the rail-head.

Now, a military rail-head is merely an ordinary average little railway station, with a spacious yard. There is nothing superficially romantic about it. It does not even mark the end of a line of railway. I have in mind one which served as the Head-quarters of a Divisional Supply Column. The organism served just one division—out of the very many divisions in France and Flanders. It was under the command of a Major. This Major, though of course in khaki and employing the same language and general code as a regimental Major, was not a bit like a regimental Major. He was no more like a regimental Major than I am myself. He had a different mentality, outlook, preoccupation. He was a man in business. He received orders—I use the word in the business sense—from the Brigades of the Division; and those orders, ever varying, had to be executed and delivered within thirty-six hours. Quite probably he had never seen a trench; I should be neither surprised nor pained to learn that he could only hit a haystack with a revolver by throwing the revolver at the haystack. His subordinates resembled him. Strategy, artillery- mathematics, the dash of infantry charges—these matters were not a bit in their line. Nevertheless, when you read in a despatch that during a prolonged action supplies went regularly up to the Front under heavy fire, you may guess that fortitude and courage are considerably in their line. These officers think about their arriving trains, and about emptying them in the shortest space of time; and they think about their motor-lorries and the condition thereof; and they pass their lives in checking lists and in giving receipts for things and taking receipts for things. Their honour may be in a receipt. And all this is the very basis of war.

My Major handled everything required for his division except water and ammunition. He would have a train full of multifarious provender, and another train full of miscellanies—from field-guns to field-kitchens—with letters from wives and sweethearts in between. And all these things came to him up the line of railway out of the sea simply because he asked for them and was ready to give a receipt for them. He was not concerned with the magic underlying their appearance at his little rail head; he only cared about the train being on time, and the lorries being in first-class running order. He sprayed out in beneficent streams from his rail-head tons of stuff every day. Every day he sent out two hundred and eighty bags of postal matter to the men beyond. The polish on the metallic portions of his numerous motor-lorries was uncanny. You might lift a bonnet and see the bright parts of the engine glittering like the brass of a yacht. Dandyism of the Army Service Corps!

An important part of the organism of the rail-head is the Railway Construction Section Train. Lines may have to be doubled. The Railway Construction Section Train doubles them; it will make new railways at the rate of several miles a day; it is self-contained, being simultaneously a depot, a workshop, and a barracks.

Driving along a road you are liable to see rough signs nailed to trees, with such words on them as "Forage," "Groceries," "Meat," "Bread," etc. Wait a little, and you may watch the Divisional Supply at a further stage. A stream of motor-lorries—one of the streams sprayed out from the rail-head—will halt at those trees and unload, and the stuff which they unload will disappear like a dream and an illusion. One moment the meat and the bread and all the succulences are there by the roadside, each by its proper tree, and the next they are gone, spirited away to camps and billets and trenches. Proceed further, and you may have the luck to see the mutton which was frozen in New Zealand sizzling in an earth-oven in a field christened by the soldiers with some such name as Hampstead Heath. The roasted mutton is a very fine and a very appetising sight. But what quantities of it! And what an antique way of cooking!

As regards the non-edible supplies, the engineer's park will stir your imagination. You can discern every device in connection with warfare. (To describe them might be indiscreet—it would assuredly be too lengthy.) . . . Telephones such as certainly you have never seen! And helmets such as you have never seen! Indeed, everything that a soldier in full work can require, except ammunition.

The ammunition-train in process of being unloaded is a fearsome affair. You may see all conceivable ammunition, from rifle cartridges to a shell whose weight is liable to break through the floors of lorries, all on one train. And not merely ammunition, but a thousand pyrotechnical and other devices; and varied bombs. An officer unscrews a cap on a metal contraption, and throws it down, and it begins to fizz away in the most disconcerting manner. And you feel that all these shells, all these other devices, are simply straining to go off. They are like things secretly and terribly alive, waiting the tiny gesture which will set them free. Officers, handling destruction with the nonchalance of a woman handling a hat, may say what they like—the ammunition train is to my mind an unsafe neighbour. And the thought of all the sheer brain-power which has gone to the invention and perfecting of those propulsive and explosive machines causes you to wonder whether you yourself possess a brain at all.

You can find everything in the British lines except the British Army. The same is to be said of the French lines; but the indiscoverability of the British Army is relatively much more striking, by reason of the greater richness and complexity of the British auxiliary services. You see soldiers—you see soldiers everywhere; but the immense majority of them are obviously engaged in attending to the material needs of other soldiers, which other soldiers, the fighters, you do not see—or see only in tiny detachments or in single units.

Thus I went for a very long walk, up such hills and down such dales as the country can show, tramping with a General through exhausting communication-trenches, in order to discover two soldiers, an officer and his man; and even they were not actual fighters. The officer lived in a dug-out with a very fine telescope for sole companion. I was told that none but the General commanding had the right to take me to that dug-out. It contained the officer's bed, the day's newspapers, the telescope, a few oddments hung on pegs pushed into the earthen walls, and, of equal importance with the telescope, a telephone. Occasionally the telephone faintly buzzed, and a very faint, indistinguishable murmur came out of it. But the orderly ignored this symptom, explaining that it only meant that somebody else was talking to somebody else. I had the impression of a mysterious underground life going on all around me. The officer's telescopic business was to keep an eye on a particular section of the German front, and report everything. The section of front comprised sundry features extremely well known by reputation to British newspaper readers. I must say that the reality of them was disappointing. The inevitable thought was: "Is it possible that so much killing has been done for such trifling specks of earth?"

The officer made clear all details to us; he described minutely the habits of the Germans as he knew them. But about his own habits not a word was said. He was not a human being—he was an observer, eternally spying through a small slit in the wall of the dug-out. What he thought about when he was not observing, whether his bed was hard, how he got his meals, whether he was bored, whether his letters came regularly, what his moods were, what was his real opinion of that dug-out as a regular home—these very interesting matters were not even approached by us. He was a short, mild officer, with a quiet voice. Still, after we had shaken hands on parting, the General, who had gone first, turned his bent head under the concealing leafage, and nodded and smiled with a quite particular cordial friendliness. "Good-afternoon, Blank," said the General to the officer, and the warm tone of his voice said: "You know—don't you, Blank?—how much I appreciate you." It was a transient revelation. As, swallowed up in trenches, I trudged away from the lonely officer, the General, resuming his ordinary worldly tone, began to talk about London music-halls and Wish Wynne and other artistes.

Then on another occasion I actually saw at least twenty fighting men! They were not fighting, but they were pretending, under dangerous conditions, to fight. They had to practise the bombing of a German trench—with real bombs. The young officer in charge explained to us the different kinds of bombs. "It's all quite safe," he said casually, "until I take this pin out." And he took the pin out. We saw the little procession of men that were to do the bombing. We saw the trench, with its traverses, and we were shown just how it would be bombed, traverse by traverse. We saw also a "crater" which was to be bombed and stormed. And that was about all we did see. The rest was chiefly hearing, because we had to take shelter behind such slight eminences as a piece of ordinary waste ground can offer. Common wayfarers were kept out of harm by sentries. We were instructed to duck. We ducked. Bang! Bang! Bang! Bang! Bang!—Bang! Then the mosquito-like whine of bits of projectile above our heads! Then we ventured to look over, and amid wisps of smoke the bombers were rushing a traverse. Strange to say, none of them was killed, or even wounded.

On still another occasion I saw a whole brigade, five or six thousand men, with their first-line transport, and two Generals with implacable eyes watching them for faults. It was a fine, very picturesque display of Imperial militancy, but too marvellously spick-and-span to produce any illusion of war. So far as I was concerned, its chief use was to furnish a real conception of numbers. I calculated that if the whole British Army passed before my eyes at the same brisk rate as that solitary and splendid brigade, I should have to stare at it night and day for about three weeks, without surcease for meals. This calculation only increased my astonishment at the obstinate in- discoverability of the Army.

Once I did get the sensation of fighting men existing in bulk. It was at the baths of a new division—the New Army. I will mention in passing that the real enthusiasm of Generals concerning the qualities of the New Army was most moving—and enheartening.

The baths establishment was very British—much more British than any of those operating it perhaps imagined. Such a phenomenon could probably be seen on no other front. It had been contrived out of a fairly large factory. It was in charge of a quite young subaltern, no doubt anxious to go and fight, but condemned indefinitely to the functions of baths-keeper. In addition to being a baths-keeper this young subaltern was a laundry-manager; for when bathing the soldiers left their underclothing and took fresh. The laundry was very large; it employed numerous local women and girls at four francs a day. It had huge hot drying-rooms where the women and girls moved as though the temperature was sixty degrees instead of being over a hundred. All these women and girls were beautiful, all had charm, all were more or less ravishing—simply because for days we had been living in a harsh masculine world—a world of motor- lorries, razors, trousers, hob-nailed boots, maps, discipline, pure reason, and excessively few mirrors. An interesting item of the laundry was a glass-covered museum of lousy shirts, product of prolonged trench-life in the earlier part of the war, and held by experts to surpass all records of the kind!

The baths themselves were huge and simple—a series of gigantic steaming vats in which possibly a dozen men lathered themselves at once. Here was fighting humanity; you could see it in every gesture. The bathers, indeed, appeared to be more numerous than they in fact were. Two hundred and fifty could undress, bathe, and re-clothe themselves in an hour, and twelve hundred in a morning. Each man of course would be free to take as many unofficial baths, in tin receptacles and so on, as he could privately arrange for and as he felt inclined for. Companies of dirty men marching to the baths, and companies of conceitedly clean men marching from the baths, helped to strengthen the ever-growing suspicion that a great Army must be hidden somewhere in the neighbourhood.

Nevertheless, I still saw not the ultimate destination of all those streams of supply which I have described.

I had, however, noted a stream in the contrary direction—that is, westwards and southwards towards the Channel and England. You can first trace the beginnings of this stream under the sound of the guns (which you never see). A stretcher brought to a temporary shelter by men whose other profession is to play regimental music; a group of men bending over a form in the shelter; a glimpse of dressings and the appliances necessary for tying up an artery or some other absolutely urgent job. That shelter is called the Aid Post. From it the horizontal form goes to (2) the Advanced Dressing Station, where more attention is given to it; and thence to (3) the Field Ambulance proper, where the case is really diagnosed and provisionally classed. By this time motor-ambulances have been much used; and the stream, which was a trickle at the Aid Post, has grown wider. The next point (4) is the Casualty Clearing Station. Casualty Clearing Stations are imposing affairs. Not until the horizontal form reaches them can an operation in the full sense of the word be performed upon it. The Clearing Station that I saw could accommodate seven hundred cases, and had held nearer eight hundred. It was housed in an extensive public building. It employed seven surgeons, and I forget how many dressers. It had an abdominal ward, where cases were kept until they could take solid food; and a head ward; and an officers' ward; immense stores; a Church of England chapel; and a shoot down which mattresses with patients thereon could be slid in case of fire.

Nearly seven hundred operations had been performed in it during the war. Nevertheless, as the young Colonel in charge said to me: "The function of a Clearing Station is to clear. We keep the majority of the cases only a few hours." Thence the horizontal forms pass into (5) Ambulance Trains. But besides Ambulance trains there are Ambulance barges, grand vessels flying the Union Jack and the Red Cross, with lifts, electric light, and an operating-table. They are towed by a tug to the coast through convenient canals.

You may catch the stream once more, and at its fullest, in (6) the splendid hospitals at Boulogne. At Boulogne the hospital laundry work is such that it has overpowered the town and has to be sent to England. But even at Boulogne, where the most solid architecture, expensively transformed, gives an air of utter permanency to the hospitals, the watchword is still to clear, to pass the cases on. The next stage (7) is the Hospital Ship, specially fitted out, waiting in the harbour for its complement. When the horizontal forms leave the ship they are in England; they are among us, and the great stream divides into many streams, just as at the rail-head at the other end the great stream of supply divides into many streams, and is lost.

Nor are men the only beings cared for. One of the strangest things I saw at Boulogne was a horse-hospital, consisting of a meadow of many acres. Those who imagine that horses are not used in modern war should see the thousands of horses tethered in that meadow. Many if not most of them were suffering from shell wounds, and the sufferers were rather human. I saw a horse operated on under chloroform. He refused to come to after the operation was over, and as I left he was being encouraged to do so by movements of the limbs to induce respiration. Impossible, after that, to think of him as a mere horse!

But before I left the British lines I did manage to glimpse the British Army, the mysterious sea into which fell and were swallowed up, and from which trickled the hundreds of small runlets of wounded that converged into the mighty stream of pain at Boulogne. I passed by a number of wooden causeways over water-logged ground, and each causeway had the name of some London street, and at last I was stopped by a complicated wall of sandbags with many curves and involutions. To "dig in" on this particular landscape is impracticable, and hence the "trenches" are above ground and sandbags are their walls. I looked through a periscope and saw barbed wire and the German positions. I was told not to stand in such-and-such a place because it was exposed. A long line of men moved about at various jobs behind the rampart of sandbags; they were cheerfully ready to shoot, but very few of them were actually in the posture of shooting. A little further behind gay young men seemed to be preparing food. Here and there were little reposing places.

A mere line, almost matching the sand-bags in colour! All the tremendous organisation in the rear had been brought into being solely for the material sustenance, the direction, and the protection of this line! The guns roared solely in its aid. For this line existed the clearing stations and hospitals in France and in Britain. I dare say I saw about a quarter of a mile of it. The Major in command of what I saw accompanied me some distance along the causeways into comparative safety. As we were parting he said:

"Well, what do you think of our 'trenches'?"

In my preoccupied taciturnity I had failed to realise that, interesting as his "trenches" were to me, they must be far more interesting to him, and that they ought to have formed the subject of conversation.

"Fine!" I said.

And I hope my monosyllabic sincerity satisfied him.

We shook hands, and he turned silently away to the everlasting peril of his post. His retreating figure was rather pathetic to me. Looking at it, I understood for the first time what war in truth is. But I soon began to wonder anxiously whether our automobile would get safely past a certain exposed spot on the high road.

## VI The Unique City

When we drew near Ypres we met a civilian wagon laden with furniture of a lower middle-class house, and also with lengths of gilt picture frame-moulding. There was quite a lot of gilt in the wagon. A strong, warm wind was blowing, and the dust on the road and from the railway track was very unpleasant. The noise of artillery persisted. As a fact, the wagon was hurrying away with furniture and picture-frame mouldings under fire. Several times we were told not to linger here and not to linger there, and the automobiles, emptied of us, received very precise instructions where to hide during our absence. We saw a place where a shell had dropped on to waste ground at one side of the road, and thrown up a mass of earth and stones on to the roof of an asylum on the other side of the road. The building was unharmed; the well-paved surface of the road was perfect—it had received no hurt; but on the roof lay the earth and stones. Still, we had almost no feeling of danger. The chances were a thousand to one that the picture-frame maker would get safely away with his goods; and he did. But it seemed odd—to an absurdly sensitive, non-Teutonic mind it seemed somehow to lack justice— that the picture-framer, after having been ruined, must risk his life in order to snatch from the catastrophe the debris of his career. Further on, within the city itself, but near the edge of it, two men were removing uninjured planks from the upper floor of a house; the planks were all there was in the house to salve. I saw no other attempt to make the best of a bad job, and, after I had inspected the bad job, these two attempts appeared heroic to the point of mere folly.

I had not been in Ypres for nearly twenty years, and when I was last there the work of restoring the historic buildings of the city was not started. (These restorations, especially to the Cloth Hall and the Cathedral of St. Martin, were just about finished in time for the opening of hostilities, and they give yet another proof of the German contention that Belgium, in conspiracy with Britain, had deliberately prepared for the war—and, indeed, wanted it!) he Grande Place was quite recognisable. It is among the largest public squares in Europe, and one of the very few into which you could put a medium-sized Atlantic liner. There is no square in London or (I think) New York into which you could put a 10,000-ton boat. A 15,000-ton affair, such as even the Arabic, could be arranged diagonally in the Grande Place at Ypres.

This Grande Place has seen history. In the middle of the thirteenth century, whence its chief edifices date, it was the centre of one of the largest and busiest towns in Europe, and a population of 200,000 weavers was apt to be uproarious in it. Within three centuries a lack of comprehension of home politics and the simple brigandage of foreign politics had reduced Ypres to a population of 5,000. In the seventeenth century Ypres fell four times. At the beginning of the nineteenth century it ceased to be a bishopric. In the middle of the nineteenth century it ceased to be fortified; and in the second decade of the twentieth century it ceased to be inhabited. Possessing 200,000 inhabitants in the thirteenth century, 5,000 inhabitants in the sixteenth century, 17400 inhabitants at the end of the nineteenth century, it now possesses 0 inhabitants. It is uninhabited. It cannot be inhabited. Scarcely two months before I saw it, the city—I was told—had been full of life; in the long period of calm which followed the bombardment of the railway-station quarter in November 1914 the inhabitants had taken courage, and many of those who had fled from the first shells had sidled back again with the most absurd hope in their hearts. As late as the third week in April the Grande Place was the regular scene of commerce, and on market-days it was dotted with stalls upon which were offered for sale such frivolous things as postcards displaying the damage done to the railway-station quarter.

Then came the major bombardment, which is not yet over.

You may obtain a just idea of the effects of the major bombardment by adventuring into the interior of the Cathedral of St. Martin. This Cathedral is chiefly thirteenth-century work. Its tower, like that of the Cathedral at Malines, had never been completed—nor will it ever be, now—but it is still, with the exception of the tower of the Cloth Hall, the highest thing in Ypres. The tower is a skeleton. As for the rest of the building, it may be said that some of the walls alone substantially remain. The choir—the earliest part of the Cathedral—is entirely unroofed, and its south wall has vanished. The apse has been blown clean out. The Early Gothic nave is partly unroofed. The transepts are unroofed, and of the glass of the memorable rose window of the south transept not a trace is left—so far as I can remember.

In the centre of the Cathedral, where the transepts meet, is a vast heap of bricks, stone, and powdery dirt. This heap rises irregularly like a range of hills towards the choir; it overspreads most of the immense interior, occupying an area of, perhaps, from 15,000 to 20,000 square feet. In the choir it rises to a height of six or seven yards. You climb perilously over it as you might cross the Alps. This incredible amorphous mass, made up of millions of defaced architectural fragments of all kinds, is the shattered body of about half the Cathedral. I suppose that the lovely carved choir-stalls are imbedded somewhere within it. The grave of Jansen is certainly at the bottom of it. The aspect of the scene, with the sky above, the jagged walls, the interrupted arches, and the dusty piled mess all around, is intolerably desolate. And it is made the more so by the bright colours of the great altar, two-thirds of which is standing, and the still brighter colours of the organ, which still clings, apparently whole, to the north wall of the choir. In the sacristy are collected gilt candelabra and other altar-furniture, turned yellow by the fumes of picric acid. At a little distance the Cathedral, ruin though it is, seems solid enough; but when you are in it the fear is upon you that the inconstant and fragile remains of it may collapse about you in a gust of wind a little rougher than usual.

You leave the outraged fane with relief. And when you get outside you have an excellent opportunity of estimating the mechanism which brought about this admirable triumph of destruction; for there is a hole made by a 17-inch shell; it is at a moderate estimate fifty feet across, and it has happened to tumble into a graveyard, so that the hole is littered with the white bones of earlier Christians.

The Cloth Hall was a more wonderful thing than the Cathedral of St. Martin, which, after all, was no better than dozens of other cathedrals. There was only one Cloth Hall of the rank of this one. It is not easy to say whether or not the Cloth Hall still exists. Its celebrated three-story facade exists, with a huge hiatus in it to the left of the middle, and, of course, minus all glass. The entire facade seemed to me to be leaning slightly forward; I could not decide whether this was an optical delusion or a fact. The enormous central tower is knocked to pieces, and yet conserves some remnant of its original outlines; bits of scaffolding on the sides of it stick out at a great height like damaged matches.

The slim corner towers are scarcely hurt. Everything of artistic value in the structure of the interior has disappeared in a horrible confusion of rubble. The eastern end of the Cloth Hall used to be terminated by a small beautiful Renaissance edifice called the Niewwerk, dating from the seventeenth century. What its use was I never knew; but the Niewwerk has vanished, and the Town Hall next door has also vanished; broken walls, a few bits of arched masonry, and heaps of refuse alone indicate where these buildings stood in April last.

So much for the two principal buildings visible from the Grande Place. The Cloth Hall is in the Grande Place, and the Cathedral adjoins it. The only other fairly large building in the Place is the Hopital de Notre Dame at the north-east end. This white-painted erection, with its ornamental gilt sign, had continued substantially to exist as a structural entity; it was defaced, but not seriously. Every other building in the place was smashed up. To walk right round the Place is to walk nearly half a mile; and along the entire length, with the above exceptions, there was nothing but mounds of rubbish and fragments of upstanding walls. Here and there in your perambulation you may detect an odour with which certain trenches have already familiarised you. Obstinate inhabitants were apt to get buried in the cellars where they had taken refuge. In one place what looked like a colossal sewer had been uncovered. I thought at the time that the sewer was somewhat large for a city of the size of Ypres, and it has since occurred to me that this sewer may have been the ancient bed of the stream Yperlee, which in some past period was arched over.

"I want to make a rough sketch of all this," I said to my companions in the middle of the Grande Place, indicating the Cloth Hall, and the Cathedral, and other grouped ruins.

The spectacle was, indeed, majestic in the extreme, and if the British Government has not had it officially photographed in the finest possible manner, it has failed in a very obvious duty; detailed photographs of Ypres ought to be distributed throughout the world.

My companions left me to myself. I sat down on the edge of a small shell-hole some distance in front of the Hospital. I had been advised not to remain too near the building lest it might fall on me. The paved floor of the Place stretched out around me like a tremendous plain, seeming the vaster because my eyes were now so much nearer to the level of it. On a bit of facade to the left the word "CYCLE " stood out in large black letters on a white ground. This word and myself were the sole living things in the Square. In the distance a cloud of smoke up a street showed that a house was burning. The other streets visible from where I sat gave no sign whatever. The wind, strong enough throughout my visit to the Front, was now stronger than ever. All the window-frames and doors in the Hospital were straining and creaking in the wind. The loud sound of guns never ceased. A large British aeroplane hummed and buzzed at a considerable height overhead. Dust drove along.

I said to myself: "A shell might quite well fall here any moment."

I was afraid. But I was less afraid of a shell than of the intense loneliness. Rheims was inhabited; Arras was inhabited. In both cities there were postmen and newspapers, shops, and even cafes. But in Ypres there was nothing. Every street was a desert; every room in every house was empty. Not a dog roamed in search of food. The weight upon my heart was sickening. To avoid complications I had promised the Staff officer not to move from the Place until he returned; neither of us had any desire to be hunting for each other in the sinister labyrinth of the town's thoroughfares. I was, therefore, a prisoner in the Place, condemned to solitary confinement. I ardently wanted my companions to come back. . . . Then I heard echoing sounds of voices and footsteps. Two British soldiers appeared round a corner and passed slowly along the Square. In the immensity of the Square they made very small figures. I had a wish to accost them, but Englishmen do not do these things, even in Ypres. They glanced casually at me; I glanced casually at them, carefully pretending that the circumstances of my situation were entirely ordinary.

I felt safer while they were in view; but when they had gone I was afraid again. I was more than afraid; I was inexplicably uneasy. I made the sketch simply because I had said that I would make it. And as soon as it was done, I jumped up out of the hole and walked about, peering down streets for the reappearance of my friends. I was very depressed, very irritable; and I honestly wished that I had never accepted any invitation to visit the Front. I somehow thought I might never get out of Ypres alive. When at length I caught sight of the Staff officer I felt instantly relieved. My depression, however, remained for hours afterwards.

Perhaps the chief street in Ypres is the wide Rue de Lille, which runs from opposite the Cloth Hall down to the Lille Gate, and over the moat water into the Lille road and on to the German lines. The Rue de Lille was especially famous for its fine old buildings. There was the Hospice Belle, for old female paupers of Ypres, built in the thirteenth century. There was the Museum, formerly the Hotel Merghelynck, not a very striking edifice, but full of antiques of all kinds. There was the Hospital of St. John, interesting, but less interesting than the Hospital of St. John at Bruges. There was the Gothic Maison de Bois, right at the end of the street, with a rather wonderful frontage. And there was the famous fourteenth-century Steenen, which since my previous visit had been turned into the post office. With the exception of this last building, the whole of the Rue de Lille, if my memory is right, lay in ruins. The shattered post office was splendidly upright, and in appearance entire; but, for all I know, its interior may have been destroyed by a shell through the roof. Only the acacia-trees flourished, and the flies, and the weeds between the stones of the paving. The wind took up the dust from the rubbish heaps which had been houses and wreathed it against what bits of walls still maintained the perpendicular. Here, too, was the unforgettable odour, rising through the interstices of the smashed masonry which hid subterranean chambers.

We turned into a side-street of small houses—probably the homes of lace-makers. The street was too humble to be a mark for the guns of the Germans, who, no doubt, trained their artillery by the aid of a very large scale municipal map on which every building was separately indicated. It would seem impossible that a map of less than a foot to a mile could enable them to produce such wonderful results of carefully wanton destruction. And the assumption must be that the map was obtained from the local authorities by some agent masquerading as a citizen. I heard, indeed, that known citizens of all the chief towns returned to their towns or to the vicinity thereof in the uniform and with the pleasing manners of German warriors. The organisation for doing good to Belgium against Belgium's will was an incomparable piece of chicane and pure rascality. Strange—Belgians were long ago convinced that the visitation was inevitably coming, and had fallen into the habit of discussing it placidly over their beer at nights.

To return to the side-street. So far as one could see, it had not received a dent, not a scratch. Even the little windows of the little red houses were by no means all broken. All the front doors stood ajar. I hesitated to walk in, for these houses seemed to be mysteriously protected by influences invisible. But in the end the vulgar, yet perhaps legitimate, curiosity of the sightseer, of the professional reporter, drove me within the doors. The houses were so modest that they had no entrance-halls or lobbies. One passed directly from the street into the parlour. Apparently the parlours were completely furnished. They were in an amazing disorder, but the furniture was there. And the furnishings of all of them were alike, as the furnishings of all the small houses of a street in the Five Towns or in a cheap London suburb. The ambition of these homes had been to resemble one another. What one had all must have. Under ordinary circumstances the powerful common instinct to resemble is pitiable. But here it was absolutely touching.

Everything was in these parlours. The miserable, ugly ornaments, bought and cherished and admired by the simple, were on the mantelpieces. The drawers of the mahogany and oak furniture had been dragged open, but not emptied. The tiled floors were littered with clothes, with a miscellany of odd possessions, with pots and pans out of the kitchen and the scullery, with bags and boxes. The accumulations of lifetimes were displayed before me, and it was almost possible to trace the slow transforming of young girls into brides, and brides into mothers of broods.

Within the darkness of the interiors I could discern the stairs. But I was held back from the stairs. I could get no further than the parlours, though the interest of the upper floors must have been surpassing.

So from house to house. I handled nothing. Were not the military laws against looting of the most drastic character! And at last I came to the end of the little street. There are many such streets in Ypres. In fact, the majority of the streets were like that street. I did not visit them, but I have no doubt that they were in the same condition. I do not say that the inhabitants fled taking naught with them. They must obviously have taken what they could, and what was at once most precious and most portable. But they could have taken very little. They departed breathless without vehicles, and probably most of the adults had children to carry or to lead. At one moment the houses were homes, functioning as such. An alarm, infectious like the cholera, and at the next moment the deserted houses became spiritless, degenerated into intolerable museums for the amazement of a representative of the American and the British Press! Where the scurrying families went to I never even inquired. Useless to inquire. They just lost themselves on the face of the earth, and were henceforth known to mankind by the generic name of "refugees"—such of them as managed to get away alive.

After this the solitude of the suburbs, with their maimed and rusting factories, their stagnant canals, their empty lots, their high, lusty weeds, their abolished railway and tram stations, was a secondary matter leaving practically no impression on the exhausted sensibility.

A few miles on the opposite side of the town were the German artillery positions, with guns well calculated to destroy Cathedrals and Cloth Halls. Around these guns were educated men who had spent years—indeed, most of their lives—in the scientific study of destruction. Under these men were slaves who, solely for the purposes of destruction, had ceased to be the free citizens they once were. These slaves were compelled to carry out any order given to them, under pain of death. They had, indeed, been explicitly told on the highest earthly authority that, if the order came to destroy their fathers and their brothers, they must destroy their fathers and their brothers: the instruction was public and historic. The whole organism has worked, and worked well, for the destruction of all that was beautiful in Ypres, and for the break-up of an honourable tradition extending over at least eight centuries. The operation was the direct result of an order. The order had been carefully weighed and considered. The successful execution of it brought joy into many hearts, high and low. "Another shell in the Cathedral!" And men shook hands ecstatically around the excellent guns. "A hole in the tower of the Cloth Hall." General rejoicing! "The population has fled, and Ypres is a desert!" Inexpressible enthusiasm among specially educated men, from the highest to the lowest. So it must have been. There was no hazard about the treatment of Ypres. The shells did not come into Ypres out of nowhere. Each was the climax of a long, deliberate effort originating in the brains of the responsible leaders. One is apt to forget all this.

"But," you say, "this is war, after all." After all, it just is.

The future of Ypres exercises the mind. Ypres is only one among many martyrs. But, as matters stand at present it is undoubtedly the chief one. In proportion to their size, scores of villages have suffered as much as Ypres, and some have suffered more. But no city of its mercantile, historical, and artistic importance has, up to now, suffered in the same degree as Ypres. Ypres is entitled to rank as the very symbol of the German achievement in Belgium. It stood upon the path to Calais; but that was not its crime. Even if German guns had not left one brick upon another in Ypres, the path to Calais would not thereby have been made any easier for the well-shod feet of the apostles of might, for Ypres never served as a military stronghold and could not possibly have so served; and had the Germans known how to beat the British Army in front of Ypres, they could have marched through the city as easily as a hyena through a rice-crop. The crime of Ypres was that it lay handy for the extreme irritation of an army which, with three times the men and three times the guns, and thirty times the vainglorious conceit, could not shift the trifling force opposed to it last autumn. Quite naturally the boasters were enraged. In the end, something had to give way. And the Cathedral and Cloth Hall and other defenceless splendours of Ypres gave way, not the trenches. The yearners after Calais did themselves no good by exterminating fine architecture and breaking up innocent homes, but they did experience the relief of smashing something. Therein lies the psychology of the affair of Ypres, and the reason why the Ypres of history has come to a sudden close.

In order to envisage the future of Ypres, it is necessary to get a clear general conception of the damage done to it. Ypres is not destroyed. I should estimate that when I saw it in July at least half the houses in it were standing entire, and, though disfigured, were capable of being rapidly repaired. Thousands of the humble of Ypres could return to their dwellings and resume home-life there with little trouble, provided that the economic situation was fairly favourable—and, of course, sooner or later the economic situation is bound to be favourable, for the simple reason that it must ultimately depend upon the exertions of a people renowned throughout the world for hard and continuous industry.

On the other hand, practically all that was spectacular in the city, all the leading, all the centre round which civic activities had grouped themselves for centuries, is destroyed. Take the Grande Place. If Ypres is to persist in a future at all comparable to its immediate past (to say nothing of its historic past), the privately owned buildings on the Grande Place will, without exception, have to be begun all over again, and before that task can be undertaken the foundations will have to be cleared—a tremendous undertaking in itself. I do not know how many privately owned buildings there were on the Grande Place, but I will guess a hundred and fifty, probably none of which was less than three stories in height. All these buildings belonged to individuals, individuals who intimately possessed them and counted on them as a source of income or well-being, individuals who are now scattered, impoverished, and acutely discouraged. The same is to be said of the Rue de Lille and of other important streets.

Suppose the Germans back again in the land of justice, modesty, and unselfishness; and suppose the property-owners of Ypres collected once more in Ypres. The enterprise of reconstruction facing them will make such a demand of initiative force and mere faith as must daunt the most audacious among them. And capital dragged out of a bankrupt Germany will by no means solve the material problem. For labour will be nearly as scarce as money; the call for labour in every field cannot fail to surpass in its urgency any call in history. The simple contemplation of the gigantic job will be staggering. To begin with, the withered and corrupt dead will have to be excavated from the cellars, and when that day comes those will be present who can say: "This skeleton was So-and-So's child," "That must have been my mother." Terrific hours await Ypres. And when (or if) the buildings have been re-erected, tenants will have to be found for them—and then think of the wholesale refurnishing! The deep human instinct which attaches men and women to a particular spot of the earth's surface is so powerful that almost certainly the second incarnation of Ypres will be initiated, but that it will be carried very far towards completion seems to me to be somewhat doubtful. To my mind the new Ypres cannot be more than a kind of camp amid the dark ruins of the old, and the city must remain for generations, if not for ever, a ghastly sign and illustration of what cupidity and stupidity and vanity can compass together when physical violence is their instrument.

The immediate future of Ypres, after the war, is plain. It will instantly become one of the show-places of the world. Hotels will appear out of the ground, guides and touts will pullulate at the railway station, the tour of the ruins will be mapped out, and the tourists and globe-trotters of the whole planet will follow that tour in batches like staring sheep. Much money will be amassed by a few persons out of the exhibition of misfortune and woe. A sinister fate for a community! Nevertheless, the thing must come to pass, and it is well that it should come to pass. The greater the number of people who see Ypres for themselves, the greater the hope of progress for mankind.

If the facade of the Cloth Hall can be saved, some such inscription as the following ought to be incised along the length of it:

"On July 31st, 1914, The German Minister At Brussels Gave A Positive And Solemn Assurance That Germany Had No Intention Of Violating The Neutrality Of Belgium. Four Days Later The German Army Invaded Belgium. Look Around."

When you are walking through that which was Ypres, nothing arouses a stronger feeling—half contempt, half anger—than the thought of the mean, miserable, silly, childish, and grotesque excuses which the wit of Germany has invented for her deliberately planned crime. And nothing arouses a more grim and sweet satisfaction than the thought that she already has the gravest reason to regret it, and would give her head not to have committed it. Despite all vauntings, all facile chatterings about the alleged co-operation of an unknowable and awful God, all shriekings of unity and power, all bellowings about the perfect assurance of victory, all loud countings of the fruits of victory—the savage leaders of the deluded are shaking in their shoes before the anticipated sequel of an outrage ineffable alike in its barbarism and in its idiocy.